CW01022039

A tranquil setting in Arnhem.

# No
# Surrender
# at Arnhem

**Robert Peatling**

Published by
Robert Peatling, 36 Park Lane
Wimborne Minster BH21 1LD

Printed and bound in Great Britain by CPI UK.

ISBN 0-9522992-1-6

ROBERT PEATLING was born in London in 1924 and followed the family tradition by becoming an apprentice compositor. On the outbreak of war, he became an ARP messenger and joined the Air Training Corps. In 1942 he was called up for army service as a tank wireless operator.

In 1943 he volunteered for parachute duties and joined 2 Para, served at Arnhem, and was Mentioned in Despatches.

He was employed in 1951 by the Daily Mirror Newspaper until his retirement in 1984. He was a caseworker for SSAFA in London and became a scout Commissioner.

He edited the history of scouting in St Albans, Hertfordshire in 1983 with his book '. . . always a Scout', and published in 1994 'Without Tradition 2 Para 1941-45', he is a member of the Wessex Branch, The Parachute Regimental Association.

# Dedication

The first dedication for this story was
written in my diary on November 19th 1944 whilst
living in a Resistance house in Arnhem.  It was
dedicated at that time to my wife and
father, a 1914-18 Middlesex Regiment soldier.
Much water has flowed under the bridge
since then and my dedication for this book must
be to the many individuals who risked
their lives to help me.
I am very sorry to record that many of them
have since passed away, three of my closest Dutch
friends, Klaas Schuttinga, brothers Martin and
John Penseel, in the German concentration camps,
before I left Holland.

# Contents

**Dedication**
*To those brave Dutch people who befriended me and paid
the supreme sacrifice.*

**Foreword**
*Lieut. Colonel (retd.) John Awdry, CO 1 Para Bn. 1959-61*

**Introduction**
*From radio operator in a tank to six jumps from a Whitley
aircraft at Ringway Aerodrome.*

# Foreword

FOR A trained journalist to try to recapture now, the daily details of a youthful adventure sixty years ago would be impossible – and if he tried, the boy would be submerged in the man.

So the appeal of this account of events during and after the struggle at Arnhem in 1944 lies in its provenance. Most of the story is the actual diary of the young Private Bob Peatling, cut off from his comrades of the 2nd Parachute Battalion, with all the fragmented understanding of events, the cheerful optimism, and even naivety of a young soldier in his first battle and its aftermath.

Even readers long familiar with the story of what befell after those ten days in September 1944 will be intrigued by the behind-the-lines observation by the boy in the attic, noting the behaviour of the German occupiers and the local citizens as they realise their first hopes of liberation are fading and German confidence is restored.

There are glimpses of good and bad on both sides and occasional sad reminders of some Dutchmen seduced by the Nordic nonsense of the Nazis, redeemed tenfold however by the conduct of others.

Then follows the evolution of the writer from hunted fugitive to successful predator, stirred by his 'ABI' (Airborne Initiative) to forage at night among his enemies for food, water, and arms.

Finally, contact at last with the Dutch Underground, the LKP. Here the story of Dutch kindness, courage and resourceful hospitality is one familiar from other accounts by 'onderdijkers' (evaders) who passed through the hands of that honoured clan. With all its frustrations, postponements, narrow escapes and at least one tragic betrayal, this was itself to be the foundation of an international friendship now sixty years long, treasured by many but by the survivors of the First Airborne Division in particular.

There is humour too. Alongside the real but somewhat mechanical sympathy of officialdom for the writer's supposed widow, there are some charming glimpses of the Pay Office, culminating in a cheque for one pound, three shillings and ninepence for 'expenses incurred whilst escaping'.

Not surprisingly, Bob Peatling's adventure ended with a well-earned Mention in Despatches. His book, which could never have been written so vividly without the recovery of the original diary (from Herman van Esveld of Kootwijkerbroek who stored it for him), deserves an equal accolade.

Lieutenant Colonel (retd.) John Awdry,
Commanding Officer, 1 Para 1959-61.

# Introduction

LIKE ALL boys born in 1924 I was called for Military service aged 18, most of us were quite happy, our parents were not. A travel voucher took me to Fulford Barracks at York where I was trained as a light infantryman by the men from the Kings Royal Rifle Company and after several ability tests, was deemed suitable to be further trained as a tank wireless operator at Barnard Castle.

After the course I noted that volunteers were required for the Glider Pilot Regiment. I volunteered and was sent for a medical by RAF Doctors at Doncaster racecourse in the summer of 1943. I failed the eye-sight test due to a stigmatism, a slight muscle problem. The Doctor saw I was disappointed and said, "if you want to fly why not join the Parachute Regiment." Why not, said this naive 19-year-old and he was in, with both feet.

I was sent to the Para training depot at Hardwick Hall, Chesterfield for several weeks of physical hell but what wonderful companions I met, every man a volunteer, I meant to succeed and not be Returned to Unit, as a good number were. At the end of this part of the training I was sent off to Ringway, Manchester airport to meet RAF Parachute Jump Instructors who softly said, "this way gentlemen". I had not been used to this politeness from Sergeants before.

We trained in the hangers, how to fall, how to land and remembered to keep feet and knees together, elbows in, hands by your ears, all simple but important rules to prevent limbs being broken on landing. Landings were not as gentle as they appear in demonstrations today, we also did not have a reserve parachute.

My first two jumps were from a tethered barrage balloon basket at 800 feet, one during the day and one at night, then another six jumps from a Whitley aircraft where you sit on the floor with your legs dangling through a four foot circular hole, one man either side ready to jump on the given order.

I passed and was presented with my red beret and the coveted wings to sew on my uniform, I felt two feet taller, "look at me Dad and paid two shillings (10p) each day extra." After that I was given a well earned two weeks leave and posted to 2nd Parachute Battalion, at Grantham who were just home from Italy to await the call to the Second Front, Europe. While we waited we trained, we had fun, and after four months in an infantry company I was transferred to our HQ company as a signaller.

There were two British Airborne Divisions, the First and the Sixth. I was in the First. The Sixth were used for D-day Normandy, while we stood to, ready in reserve for any situation that arose. There were many such calls like Caen and Falaise, one that stands out in my mind was on the 15th August, we had been briefed to drop west of Paris, Rambouillet. Just think! First troops into Paris, I had never been there before. We slept on the airfield at RAF Down Ampney with our 'chutes as pillows, the operation was postponed then cancelled.

On the 31st August we were briefed for operation LINNET, to take and hold some bridges on the Belgium border, that was cancelled. This was becoming a habit; seven days later 7th September we were briefed for operation COMET, to drop on a bridge on the south bank of the Rhine at a town called Arnhem in Holland, yes, that was cancelled. Some days later we were told, take five days leave but be back to Stoke Rochford by 2359 hours on Friday without fail, the operation would be on this time. Yes we had stragglers but I have never heard of a man who missed the roll call in 2 Para.

On Saturday morning the companies A, B, C, HQ & Support came to Stoke Rochford for briefing, using a sand table relief map, each platoon was shown its Drop Zone (DZ) and objectives. This was a very exciting time for a 20 year old Private soldier who had never been to war before, we were off to a town on the Rhine to hold a bridge for 48 hours until the army, 64 miles away, relieved us.

It did not work out that way, on Wednesday 20th September I found myself alone in a Police station in the centre of Arnhem waiting for an overdue army to arrive.

I looked for a notebook to write a letter home, after a few days the notebook was filled, I found a new ledger book and entered the date each day, the ledger became a diary, that was good, for surely none of my comrades would believe the story I would tell when they arrive, today or tomorrow. I kept that diary until the 31st December 1944, three and a half months after starting that letter. It was now very dangerous to carry around so I left it with a trustworthy farmer, Herman van Esveld at Kootwijkerbroek, near Barneveld for safe keeping. When he was liberated by the Canadian army late in April 1945, he handed it to an Officer. In August 1945 I received two letters from the MI9 at the War Office saying they have my diary and to attend for interrogation in London and to collect my diary. That is what you will be reading.

There is a downside to the story, my wife was notified by the Record Office that I was Missing from the 25th September.

I was still missing after the regulation six months and my wife was sent a War Widow's Pension of ten shillings a week (50p). She did not draw it for she was quite sure I would come home.

I had great difficulty in finding an apt title for the book, MISSING WITHOUT TRACE was one possibility and then I re-read the citation for my Mention in Despatches. One paragraph read:

> ***Despite the lack of food and companionship, and the temptation that by giving himself up he would be able to write to his wife, PEATLING never wavered in his decision not to surrender to the enemy.*** (WO373/101).

That makes *NO SURRENDER at ARNHEM* a natural choice of title.

# Paſſierſchein

Der deutſche Soldat, der dieſen Paſſierſchein vorzeigt, benutzt ihn als Zeichen ſeines ehrlichen Willens, ſich zu ergeben. Er iſt zu entwaffnen. Er muß gut behandelt werden. Er hat Anſpruch auf Verpflegung und, wenn nötig, ärztliche Behandlung. Er wird ſo bald wie möglich aus der Gefahrenzone entfernt.

*Dwight D Eisenhower*

**OBERBEFEHLSHABER**
der alliierten Expeditions-Armeen

*Englische Übersetzung nachstehend. Sie dient
als Anweisung an die alliierten Vorposten.*

# SAFE CONDUCT

The German soldier who carries this safe conduct is using it as a sign of his genuine wish to give himself up. He is to be disarmed, to be well looked after, to receive food and medical attention as required, and to be removed from the danger zone as soon as possible.

*Dwight D Eisenhower*

**SUPREME COMMANDER,**
Allied Expeditionary Force

Leaflet dropped near Arnhem by the RAF.
Given to me by Nico from his day-book of events.

# CHAPTER ONE

## 17 September 1944

*This transcript is taken from a notebook written as a letter to my wife. It was started on Wednesday 20 September, 1944, while I waited for our troops to arrive, take Arnhem and relieve us from our desperate hold on the north end of the main bridge. I had no idea of the dire events that had occurred within the Division and the rest of the supposedly successful British 2nd Army coming up from Belgium. My letter was purposely left very sparing of information about what had happened to me on the first three days at Arnhem. I have now filled in the gaps.*

IT WAS a glorious sunny morning as we waited to board the planes. Quite an inspiring sight to see so many parachutists, with their equipment, standing by to have a bash at Jerry. Tea and sandwiches were obtainable from a wagon that came round to the various aircraft.

The American crew of my plane said they had a lot of experience, this being their sixth time for dropping paratroops on operations. We were all keyed up, yet I could not imagine myself in a strange country, fighting, within a few hours.

The time came to set off and we donned our equipment and 'chutes, took up positions for emplaning and that was to be the last time I touched British soil for longer than any of us could have anticipated.

We took off and cruised around for the planes to get into a correct formation and then headed straight for Holland.

From the air I enjoyed the view of the beautiful green countryside of England. There were several small boats around just off the coast; they seemed unconcerned with the sky full of slow lumbering aircraft. We met some light anti-aircraft fire as we crossed into Holland, some fields were already flooded by the Germans and we saw some of our gliders in fields, few and far between.

Not enough praise can be given to our fighter pilots who followed us in, shooting-up light anti-aircraft guns on river boats and keeping good watch over their convoy. In the plane I was sitting next to Lieutenant Tom Ainslie who was to jump number five and I was number six.

Some weeks before while we were under canvas on an airfield waiting for an operation in France, Mr. Ainslie's batman had told me he was not going on that one. He was an old hand in the platoon, well respected, married with two children and had been on two operations, Oudna and Sicily. Both operations had sustained many casualties. The French operation was cancelled and the next morning he was not to be found.

The following week the Platoon Sergeant, Bill Cloves M.M. a regular soldier and the one who had wanted me to leave "A" Company to join his signal platoon, suggested that as I was the last man into his platoon, would I stand in for the missing batman until his return? I had no hesitation in saying that was not for me. I was not in the Battalion to polish brasses and leathers. He left it at that, but two days later was back with another line of thought. The batman would be sure to return soon and the Officer was the best type he had ever worked with, would I please have a word with Mr. Ainslie and I could tell him it was just temporary. I did. He was a Cambridge classic scholar and I have never met a finer gentleman. The result was that I agreed to take the assignment.

Now, back to our aircraft approaching the drop zone. Sgt. Major Bishop was at the end of the Dakota aircraft jumping last, number 24.

At a given signal we stood in line and watched until the red light went off, the green appeared, and the Sgt. Major pushed everyone forward from the back to make sure that they jumped closely so he did not have a long walk back to the rendezvous point (RV). It must have been the tightest stick I have ever experienced; nobody had a chance to say, "Leave me out this time!"

We landed on a ploughed field at Heelsum around 13.45 hours. I made for the yellow flare that was the Battalion RV, I was OK and so was my kit.

Our signallers were attached to the other companies and they all reported in to HQ, 98% down and ready. Our Commanding Officer gave the word for "A" Company to move off for the objective and HQ Company followed.

About a dozen prisoners were taken very quickly. "A" Company took the lead and we were held up at times due to some machine guns covering the road crossings, and to some persistent snipers. I could hardly believe my eyes when I saw my first dead comrade, placed on a low garden wall with his eyes closed and his arms folded across his chest, as if asleep.

The first German casualties were a horrific sight. A small German staff car had been travelling along the road towards us and everything opened up on them. When I reached them the driver was out of the car, dead, and the officer was sprawled headfirst out of the open door. Both were riddled with bullets. The day of make-believe was over. This was the real thing.

Our casualties were minimal. Wally Rook had injured his ankle and, being the Colonel's wireless operator, was put on a jeep to continue into town. I met "Tich" Kirlow, from Castleford, who, after completing training with me, had volunteered for the Independent Company. He told me that Dennis Portman, my close friend was coming over with our spare wireless sets in a glider the following day.

The reaction from the Dutch people was wonderful. We were treated as liberators. Outside nearly every house was a container of apples, pears, tomatoes and buckets of water. At some houses milk was offered. I thought such scenes only happened at the cinema. We had marched eight miles on a warm day, with full equipment, under fire at times. A very exciting day!

The Dutch railway drivers had been told to strike on the Sunday we arrived and there was a train stopped, with no passengers, by the railway bridge, one mile from the centre of Arnhem.

The railway bridge was the objective of "C" Company and the first section of men raced on to it when a loud explosion and smoke announced that the Germans had blown one of the spans. Private Sadler was shot by a sniper and Lt. Peter Barry was wounded. I was on the road above the bridge watching the excitement unravel. The enemy's demolition of the railway bridge was very unfortunate for we were then unable to get a platoon across the river to take the south end of the main Arnhem road bridge.

We took control of the north end of the road bridge, with the Germans at the south end and, although there were determined efforts to dislodge the enemy, we suffered casualties without being able to get near enough to them to be effective.

Lt. Ainslie called me to join him on a reconnaissance to find "B" Company somewhere up on high ground back along the road we had travelled. We went, amongst a din of Bren and rifle fire, "freezing" every time someone put up an illuminating flare which made everywhere brighter than daylight, or so it seemed. Eventually we raised "B" Company on the radio to bring them in.

On our return there was much activity and CSM Bishop told me to accompany Major Wallis (the second in command of the Battalion), to look for boats to enable us to cross the river and get some men over on the south side and so take that end of the bridge.

We made off back towards the railway bridge, scouring the water's edge for a boat in the inky darkness without success, when the Germans on the south side opened up with tracer bullets onto the stone walls of the bank of the river below us. Major Wallis was just behind me.

I went flat on the road and fired back at the source of the annoyance, two-thirds of the way along the enormous metal bridge. The firing stopped and I continued on my way. I called for my officer, but I had now lost contact with him.

Major Wallis, a tall elegant officer, had walked that time with only a walking stick in his hand, his revolver remained in its holster, absolutely fearless and unconcerned by the noise and excitement going on around him. It does help to have such cool company. That left me on my own, in pitch darkness, obviously thinking that Major Wallis was ahead, still looking for those boats. He surely wouldn't return without completing his mission? So on I went, looking, gently calling out and altogether not very happy with my lot. Blame the Sergeant Major!

After reaching a natural rise from the lower river frontage to the road above, and not finding Major Wallis, I decided it would be better to return to base at the bridge and started carefully walking back. Very soon I heard the sound of marching feet and took up a firing position in a large doorway concealed up about six steps. I made out the shape of our own men and called out to the first man who was a Sergeant of the brigade military police. We studied a town map and he suggested that, for safety I join him on the return. I could drop off as soon as any second battalion chaps challenged us.

They were taking a number of German POWs through to the police station in Arnhem and, according to the map, we would be in the area of the second battalion. I agreed.

We made the police station without incident. The police were thrilled with our presence but this was not the place for me or for Sgt. Harry Parker from the third Battalion. A Lieutenant Morley had arrived to check his men so I told him two of us were off back to our Battalion at the bridge. He said: "No, stay here for the present, I will bring a patrol for you later this morning". So we waited.

By morning light our Sergeant had made a very good assessment of the situation and had us posted all round the building to cover us from attack from any direction. In my position on the first floor of the police President's room, I had a good view of the crossroads in a shopping area, and I saw more Germans than I imagined could exist.

We did not have a Bren gun with us, only Stens and rifles. The Sergeant said we would wait while we were not discovered until our chaps could make the attack up the road from the bridge, then we would ambush Jerry from the rear.

One of our lads had left his small pack on a table in the policemen's locker room. The Sergeant and I happened to be there as Jerry came along, one of them saw the pack through a window, broke the glass and two climbed in. We eased ourselves gently through a doorway, closing a door. Sergeant Callaway gave his orders to me: "If they attempt to come through that door, kill them both", and he went off and left me to it!

Knowing how unreliable a Sten gun could be just when you need it, I was more than a little apprehensive. What is more it was the first time that I was called upon to shoot a human being at close range, in cold blood. It is something I shall never forget; I would not wish that duty on any man. But, it had to be faced.

We kept the POWs quiet, although they were very hungry by now and we decided to move out when all went quiet and make our way down to the bridge. Wrapping our boots in pieces of blanket in the pitch-blackness, we each found a

The immaculate Police Station when I arrived with the prisoners and the military police. I stayed alone for six weeks

20

comfortable spot. And so, in our exhausted state, slept. It was beginning to get light when I awoke. We decided to stay another day. I was not sorry, surely our chaps would link up with us today? At first light the enemy was passing our building continually on the way to the bridge, with spasmodic firing from the south.

On two occasions Jerry entered through the open gates of the police station. Our man on that post opened fire, sending them on their way pretty sharply. They did not return the fire, or call for help. We were quite surprised. They obviously had orders to make for the bridge, about 300 yards to the south, and they were not going to be diverted.

That evening we decided to leave the prisoners locked up in the cells and move off back to the bridge. We had the idea of taking some prisoners, as safe escort through their lines. We closed the outer doors to stop Jerry using our place as a headquarters for their vehicles, or for a resting-place, and waited for the traffic to subside.

There was still spasmodic firing going on around, but we were optimistic that our chaps would be through to us that day. Only one policeman had been near us since they went off duty in the early hours of Monday morning.

I was surprised to see the different German uniforms, of many colours, grey, blue, black and green. They did not appear to be good smart soldiers and were of a wide variety of age groups. The young prisoners that we had taken on arrival had sores on their legs.

We made the hungry prisoners some tea, and gave them a biscuit each. I was very hungry myself and one of the lads gave me some biscuits. Our nerves were on edge by this time for one of the prisoners had screamed out "Englanders" to a passing German and we were scared that Jerry would discover us before nightfall. One group of Germans did try to come in. The first man was shot in the shoulder and the small group ran off and did not return.

The town was now crammed full with Germans and guns and we thought Jerry would want to use the police station to garrison some of his troops, for their barracks were bombed on Sunday by the RAF and set on fire. I made friends with the chaps who were there with me. Wally Whitmill was a Corporal with the brigade military police, and he said he was not going to be taken prisoner. He was an experienced soldier and served in North Africa, I decided to keep an eye on him. I could not see any way out, certainly not over the roof. Sgt. Harry Parker was at the forefront of any trouble, I felt very fortunate to have these chaps with me in this situation.

The police station was in an excellent strategic position, a detached building in the centre of a square, with wide entrances onto the road. There was only one room looking out onto the road at the back and that was at half-basement level and easily covered. The POWs were in cells backing onto this back street and, whenever they heard German voices, shouted out as loud as they could. It's a good job we were British or they would have been shot.

We could see the shopping centre down the road being looted by civvies and Germans alike during any lull in the fighting. Armfuls of shoes from the Bata shop opposite were being carried away. Some women were linking arms with the German soldiers and seemed very pleased they were in Arnhem.

One policeman called back to see how we were coping. One German soldier saw a wireless set by a downstairs front window, broke the window and scooped the set out.

Then came our downfall. All had gone quiet when five civilians walked boldly into the side garage entrance, they were challenged and brought back inside, much to their surprise. Some would have shot them but, after consultation, it was agreed to let them go as we were promised they would bring some food back.

Fifteen minutes later we knew our cover was blown. At the far end of the road, near the barracks, an open lorry with the same size trailer, full of German infantrymen, came slowly down the road to our position. What sounded like a mortar bomb exploded in the yard and our chaps started firing at the foot soldiers left in the road. Sergeant Callaway shouted, "Stop firing and give yourselves up". He then walked out of the first floor room, threw down his Sten gun and walked down the stone staircase with his hands up. I was behind him, but instead of going down with the others I flew like the wind up a narrow wooden staircase to the attic, thinking I stood a chance of escaping or I might be shot if they find me.

The thought of being a POW horrified me. The Germans made the noisiest assault I have ever heard or witnessed. They were not from the sick, lame and lazy battalion, they were Panzer Grenadiers and one left, on the staircase, a forage cap with a skull and crossbones badge. I had never been so scared in all my life as at that moment. They fired into every room, shouted what could have been "Englander, Swinehound, Kameradie", whatever it was, it did not sound very friendly to me. The eight military policemen were taken prisoner, our German prisoners were released and I was left to sweat it out in the attic.

It was not until a few days later when I looked outside the main door, I saw Sgt. Callaway on the pavement, dead. He had been shot as he gave himself up. He is buried in the

The Police station after I left, in an iron corset to prevent it falling down. Some years later it was demolished.

Oosterbeek cemetery. I am glad I did not join him when he called out for me to follow. I knew in my heart why I took the chance to escape. My father had been a Middlesex Regiment man in the 1914-18 conflict in France and would not look kindly at his son being made prisoner by those bloody Germans.

I quickly hauled myself up on the rafters of this large open attic. In one corner was a wooden locked shed, about 8' x 10', with a flat roof. The position gave a good view of anyone entering the attic. The whole area was fitted with shelving and was full of confiscated wireless sets. My .38 army issue revolver was at my side for I was reckoning on a point-blank range. Better than relying on the unreliable Sten gun. The firing had stopped. They must have taken our prisoners from the cellars and our chaps with them. I had a strange feeling I had won the first round!

Once Jerry had left I took stock. Whit had brought his small pack up here during one of the many previous alarms. It contained his washing gear, a full water bottle, four biscuits and a meat block. I had my emergency chocolate and so I was OK for a couple of days until our chaps came up this far into Arnhem. Just before dusk I carefully crept downstairs to look for a bucket of water to have a good wash. I was unlucky, the water was off. As darkness fell I took off my boots for the first time and, with my jump smock to sleep on, slept until morning, despite the noise.

# CHAPTER TWO

# Wednesday 20 September 1944

*Alone and hungry but not downhearted, Monty promised we would be relieved in 24 hours and home for Christmas!*

I DECIDED the best way to pass the time would be to write a diary of my previous escapade and back I went upstairs for a note book and pencil and have been writing all this morning. It seems strange that I go regularly to the latrine and yet have not had anything substantial to eat since Saturday. I don't seem hungry only very thirsty for it is very stuffy in this attic. My mouth is foul but I cannot spare the water. I was lucky always carrying my tooth brush with me for with Whits S.R. toothpaste it quite refreshes the mouth.

The water I have smells horrid I only hope the army break through tomorrow and the bridge is still intact. I hope when Jerry retreats he doesn't use this place as a strong point for I will be in a hot spot all round. I have enough food to last me for another 2 days (with plenty of sleep). Needless to say I am not in favour of close contact action.

Jerry is putting up an intense ack ack barrage against our aircraft and I am in a ridiculous position for protection against shelling or bombing. This is the first time I have witnessed bombing other than London.

I have had my dinner a small mug of Oxo and shall have some tea tonight. I am getting fed up with hearing German voices and hope to wake up in the morning and hear a British C.S.M. blaspheming at his children in the approved style. I am going barmy keeping up a conversation with myself in a whisper.

This attic is full of wireless sets collected from the local residents, so it wasn't propaganda after all, wireless sets were confiscated. Our troops should have captured the ground 15 miles south of here and the army proper had about 64 miles to go to reach us last Saturday, so they can't be so far off.

It is a terrible suspense waiting for time to pass and left to my own thoughts. I wonder if all the other nine chaps said comrade on Tuesday. I shall enquire as soon as I get back myself for we were spread over four different parts of the building and one or two may have hidden like me.

There were eight from the Brigade Provost Staff, one from the Third Battalion and myself, this Harry Parker from the other Battalion was particularly game, he wanted to go alone and bring back his section for the prisoners, he was a great inspiration for me, all these other chaps had been in action before except me.

I should be happier if only I could get more water for I could drink it by the gallon in this stuffy atmosphere.

There is artillery firing about 50 yards from here and every time it fires a succession of broken windows follows. When Jerry was downstairs looking for the Englander swinehounds he put bullets into everywhere for destruction, a beautiful marble clock was used as a target for an automatic, vases were smashed, doors, windows, everything within reach.

I now reckon to make food last me until Saturday with my emergency chocolate and then Sunday night take to the roads and hope for the best. For water I shall have to take some from the lavatory cistern for since the big fires of Monday evening all the water has been cut off. Whit had some water sterilizer tablets so I must use them.

What annoys me about losing my small pack is that there were three bars of Lifebuoy soap, three apples, 40 Players, a lovely meat sandwich on top of an unopened 48 hour ration which includes six bars of chocolate and three-quarter pound of boiled sweets. All of which would be very welcome now.

I bet the lads will be surprised at seeing me once I get back. I only hope that Joan hasn't been notified that I am missing for I know how much she will worry.

As I write there are no end of bangs, for our aircraft are

overhead and the ack ack is terrific. I feel quite safe perched up here because it is our lads doing the bombing. I have some good news for our Intelligence officer if he hurries up, of the condition of Jerry's troops, most of them are footsore and all the prisoners we had were suffering from scabs and sores on their legs. I am hoping this bombing is a prelude to a night attack.

I feel quite a hero in myself quite happy but definitely in need of some solid food. All the civvies at home have had a rough time with the bombing and I have had quite a safe time in the army.

## Thursday 21 September 1944

Things certainly look black today for Jerry is in occupation here and is using the yard as a garage. I wonder how they would take it if they knew an Englander Swinehound was in the building, I don't suppose they would be amused in the least, no sense of humour. This should make quite a historic diary but personally I would rather play the quiet stay at home lad.

I haven't really enough water for today only about an inch in my water bottle. There is no noise of any firing whatsoever. I can't make it out. Field Marshal Montgomery has dropped a clanger over Arnhem but me a bigger one, I have no doubt mine can be heard ringing in Green Lanes Harringay now. I took the skylight off the roof last night and the whole panorama south by the riverside was a vivid orange and red, just like the 1940 Fire of London.

I keep hoping for the sight of a Sherman tank but all in vain up to the moment. Everyday I keep hoping for the morrow, but today everything does rely on the morrow for my water situation is critical. Isn't it strange that everything should happen to me for example why do I get mixed up with a section of MPs that are taken prisoner?

At nights I am having some beautiful dreams, from Dad cutting me piles of deliciously thin ham sandwiches to finding crates of wine downstairs.

There is still no noise of firing, so I presume the lads have taken the boat for England, don't I wish I was on that boat, my first job would be a Dettol bath.

Aircraft fly over spasmodically but that isn't any good to me, although a 12,000 lb Block-buster might take me to my own lines, I'd even risk that rather than these circumstances. I long for 8pm each evening when it gets dark then I can do plenty of observing without much chance of being discovered. 3pm - I have made three attempts this afternoon to reach the fire extinguisher on the next floor but each time been frustrated by movements in my direction.

The ten of us could never have held on at this place for Jerry must be using it as an advanced HQ according to the number of vehicles that keep stopping outside. I have thought of going down and shooting the General but on second thoughts my life is worth more than his.

The soldiers in steel helmets have disappeared so it looks as though the front is miles away. The water I managed to get from the fire extinguisher smells most horrid and though I have boiled it and used sterilizer tablets on it, it is not fit to drink.

As soon as it gets dusk I'll see if the lads left any rations around the building, if so I'll wait, otherwise I'll try and get to the troops myself. All the civilians are walking around in white coats and waving white flags (I wish I had a camera). Some optimistic ones are clearing up after the bombing and looting. Jerry seems to be doing a lot of patrolling on motor-bikes. If I thought I could trust any of the civilians I would confide in one.

I made a marvellous discovery downstairs of a water set, it made one and a half glasses, I gulped it down greedily and came out in a sweat almost immediately. I do hope the lads come tomorrow for I am just about all in, my stomach has ached all day through lack of food. I want to do something, I hate lying doggo like this.

**Friday 22 September 1944**
Life is full of pleasant surprises for during the night I managed to get a water bottle full of water from the lavatory cistern downstairs. I was so thirsty I drank two mugfuls

without sterilising. I awoke this morning to find three coppers up here examining the damage, they took my clock downstairs with them.

Last night I managed to recover my equipment, steel helmet and three magazines for Whits sten. Once again last night there was a large fire blazing on the waterfront. All the civilians are packing their belongings and moving north for there is no water, gas or electricity in the town.

It is a pitiful sight to see them trudging behind hand carts. Tomorrow must be my last day here for I only have a biscuit left and am feeling the pangs of hunger considerably, so just for my sake I hope they break through. The Brigadier wants to get cracking with his O Group.

Jerry certainly had a find with my pals as prisoners, for the Sergeant had binoculars, three had .38 revolvers, all had stens and quite a few wristwatches. When the Germans saw hand grenades in the pouches on the equipment they left them alone, I believe they are really scared of our Mills 36.

If only Monty would put one of his 40 mile a day spear-heads into operation in this direction life would be much easier. NO! I suppose he is sitting back having his morning coffee – still I should be at NAAFI myself.

I really can't make out what has happened that the army is so long in coming, they only had about 64 miles at the outside to reach the nearest paratroops, although I realise crossing three independent rivers is no joke.

Our aircraft are over on a considerable scale today and meeting heavy ack ack quite different from that we met when entering Holland. I wondered as I crossed the British Coast how long it would be before I saw it again, I have my doubts now if ever I shall see it.

I think I'll demand a Court of Inquiry into this matter when I return. I have no idea what the time is since the coppers took my clock downstairs and I can't go down there for they are there still. I have no doubt in my mind that the Allies will take over sooner or later but I am a little bothered about the sooner part. I'd love to see a great big Sherman come rumbling past with its white Star shining. I hope my Guv'nor hasn't found himself another Batman for I should hate to lose him now. I must get back for I owe him a £1 and I'd hate to be in debt to such an excellent chap.

I am craving for the sound of rifle fire again and the charge from Paddy Hannan's bugle. I can't help thinking of Phipsy roughing it as a rifleman with a duty company. I wonder if Mr Grayburn is an MC yet? (He won a posthumous Victoria Cross). What would he do in this position? I hope Harry Kingwell is still plodding along with his snipers rifle, I wish there were more chaps like him in this world.

I suppose the civvies at home are thinking Arnhem is a long time being taken, and thinking the army must be having a rest. Oh how hard done by they are with income tax and a 54 hour week, some even longer, just give me a chance to change with them. I wonder how long it will be before we dine at the Rookery Nook and go off to the Cameo or to the Royal for a dance once again, about Christmas I hope.

I have just had a near escape for three coppers came dashing upstairs without any warning. I flew across the beams like a scared rabbit, they had a couple of workmen with them and look like starting repairs on the roof soon. My spirits are low today, I do wish there would be some bombing to liven things up and help pass the time.

A crowd of Jerrys have just marched by singing very gustily of their Fatherland, just wait until they hear of the Motherland. There is a woman in the yard crying her eyes out for some reason and at times yelling or bellowing at the coppers, something obviously has upset her, she has been like it for half an hour now.

At last something has happened, the fighters have been over and dropped two bombs apiece, already six have shaken this building but I can stand it so long as the boys get here tomorrow. I have a little chocolate left so will make some cocoa as all my water must be boiled before drinking. I find that anything hot quenches the thirst much better than cold. Tonight once again I shall go exploring for more water, that is if the coppers clear out.

It will be lovely to hear English spoken once again. One

of the coppers must be called Petas or the like for I keep thinking someone is calling me. Another must be Engely and sounds like Dutch for Englishman.

I think I have reason to be fed up, miles from a friend, dead scared to be seen by one of these gabbling foreigners, no food to eat and only cistern water to drink, but cheered with the thought that tomorrow will be my D Day. The Dutch girls are not bad looking but the men are tall and thin like some Yanks. They do wear clogs still, but were dressed extremely smartly on that Sunday we arrived.

## Saturday 23 September 1944

During the night I was lucky to get a jug of water, I guzzled the water bottle while perched out on the roof last night. One copper came up just as I was boiling some water this morning so I just laid flat on the opposite shed, one stole my steel helmet as a protection against shrapnel I suppose, it is a wonder they have not thought of stripping my equipment for my belt.

I felt weak in the arms and legs last night although it can't be wondered at for I have only eaten a bare 24 hour ration in a week. There was a quarter moon up last night and very clear sky, tanks seemed to be on the move through town according to the rumblings I heard. I shall have to do something tomorrow night unless I can live on a limited quantity of hot water.

Most of the civilians are now out of town and only Jerry and some coppers seem to be left. I have now decided, that to try and leave town on Sunday night would be giving myself up, for all civilians are off the streets by dusk and Jerry patrols on motor bikes, so my plan of campaign is to stay here and look for my opportunity to go or die of starvation.

It sounds so degrading to think of being a Prisoner in German hands, besides I want to see England and Joan before the end of the war. It is the unknown that makes people give in but being a staunch believer in fate and faith I am going to hang on.

I remember reading of chaps marching and one gave in after a long march with only five minutes to go and he did not know it.

If our troops are not through by Monday I think I shall leave here on Tuesday morning while still dark and risk asking a Hollander (as they call themselves) for food. I have written on a piece of paper, Can you hide me, I am English, I am hungry and thirsty, how much do I owe you? Taken from a Dutch/English paper we were issued.

A Jerry has just shot a dog, he injured it with the first shot and took six more shots to put it out of its misery. They are inhuman these bastards. All the coppers have photos of Adolph hanging in their rooms, so they need replacing.

### Sunday 24 September 1944

I wonder why we did not hold the bridge last week. I suppose we thought Jerry was away on a 36 hour pass and positions were not necessary. I must not be sour. The bombing and shelling was intense last night and several times I thought my last moment had come.The coppers did not come in until 1.30pm today so I suppose they went to mass this morning.

I seem to be getting very thin for my hip bones stick out and make it very difficult for sleeping. It will be nice to get these trousers off once again. I found a map of Europe from one of the rooms downstairs and find that I am due East of London and twice as far again from Berlin, the shorter distance will suit me thank you! What a Sunday afternoon, pouring with rain and nothing to eat. My blood is beginning to run thin for these last few nights I have shivered on my bed.

The ack ack has stopped and things are melancholy and quiet. General Dempsey only had 64 miles to go. I could have walked there and back in a week. I only wish I could try now. I dreamt last night that Ginger Perry of the Signals woke me up and said Hey, don't you want your haversack rations? I'd tuck into an army sandwich as if it were a relish now. So altogether I did not enjoy my sleep on an empty stomach. I am a weeks money to credit, an unheard of occurrence, I suppose I shall be quite a few before I ever collect any again.

I fully realise that Holland has many natural defences but that is no reason why I am left here like a lemon. If I was in England this pleasant Sunday afternoon, no doubt I would be on a weekend leave. There were very few weekends I missed from March until September, except during exercises and the invasion crisis. The ack ack was terrific last night, I suppose the RAF bombed Germany.

One of my treasures is a small china bulldog I found, I think I'll show that spirit and hang on until the lads arrive.

Really I think last Tuesday was the luckiest day in my life that Jerry did not look up here for the Englander Swinehound. It gets under my skin to hear that expression. When I meet Mr Ainslie I think he had better look after me rather than me him in future.

This is certainly a queer situation waiting for one army to push another back. Jerry is definitely in the best position only having a few miles of communications to his own country and all our supplies about 400 miles by land and sea. It will be dreadful if we have been pushed back into Belgium as I dreamt last night. I wonder how near the battle will get before I can hear it. I tried signalling to our aircraft with a mirror and the sun but I suppose they thought it a skylight reflecting, not that they can do anything for me.

At this rate the Russians will be here first. I don't know whether that would be good or bad. I stole about 60 cents from downstairs for my money is no good until the British take possession. No doubt I'll be on a charge for opening my Emergency Ration without an Officer's permission.

A jeep has just pulled up outside here, but I am sorry to say in Jerry's hands; it still has the white star on the front and sides.

I have done a lot of thinking today and have decided to go North to the railway and then North West in the direction of Ede, hoping to get in with an elderly family, not German minded. It is only the food situation that makes me go. I don't think the coppers would be very kind hearted for I tore up their blankets for pads last Monday. I must shave before I go for I look a good imitation of the wild man from Borneo, not having shaved for well over a week. I hope they don't make a pocket around Arnhem like Falaise and pound away until they give in.

### Monday 25 September 1944

It was a marvellous sunny evening which turned into a clear moonlight night just right for a spin on the old motor bike. I found another blanket from downstairs and am using that under me to keep me warm. I keep saying to myself I shall be relieved for the sound of our planes gives me every encouragement.

I feel as if I would kill for a loaf of bread I feel that hungry I have just had a taste now of all the crumbs in my ration box, crumbs of chocolate, meat, salt and biscuits all to make water tastier.

I am much more concerned over Joan worrying about me missing than going into a Prisoner of War camp for about a year, for while laying on my bed deep in thought, I was thinking of Joan receiving the War Office notice that I was missing and shed some tears for I know how all at home will be upset at hearing that.

Here I am Monday afternoon without a morsel to eat. Am I downhearted? I'll say I am! Jerry's vehicles and his equipment is far below our standard so there is no reason why the boys should not be here by now. I look very white and thin faced after shaving. Jerry is in a variety of coloured uniforms. Black, green, grey and some khaki.

Since last writing I now have a pipe and tobacco I found downstairs so shall try and keep hunger away with smoking. The fighters have had a glorious day zooming down on the ack ack barrage and quite encouraged me. Opposite is a warehouse Van der Harts and two lorries and about 50 Jerrys are looting all the materials from it, great rolls of cloth, underclothes, dresses and coats are coming out. There is a Bata shop next to that and that is supplying shoes for all, none of the soldiers seem at all interested in the war. I am getting into the habit of staying under the blanket each morning till about 10am and then the day passes quicker, my first job on meeting our forces will be to send a Field Card home. Grandmother always said her Roman Catholic charm would bring me luck and a safe return to her, I hope so in this instance, tomorrow for preference.

*(This day General Urquhart received orders to withdaw his Division back over the Rhine during the night. 2136 men were successful, an 80% casualty rate. Only 17 men from 2 Para, out of the 501 who landed ten days previously, made it).*

### Tuesday 26 September 1944

Today will see the completion of one week of solitude and I celebrated by finding a little tea and sugar cube in the cells where we brewed up last week, it is enough for two small mugs.

Up to the present I have always hoped for tomorrow but as Mother always said tomorrow never comes, so now I hope for Thursday when I really must go. I have had my first hot meal for eleven days – a bowl of soup. I was rummaging about in the cupboards downstairs and found two packets of soup, some tea crackers and a little rank butter and two small apples. I immediately used one packet of soup for a pint of soup and some crackers.

I feel certain of pulling through. It only needs patient waiting. I must obtain water from somewhere as soon as it becomes dark. There is no doubt about soup being warming to the blood for I feel all of a glow inside, but I really need something solid like potatoes. They don't grow in the middle of a town so shall have to want, I am afraid. Surely Monty has thought up something in ten days. I'd give him a talking to if he was here now.

If only I could hitch-hike on one of these planes I don't think I would report for quite a few days.

### Wednesday 27 September 1944

I wonder if the lads are a days fighting nearer to Arnhem, or at a standstill. I'd love to look at a newspaper now to see how the war is progressing. I am sorry to write there was no air activity last night but it has resumed again this morning. I saw a Jerry on one of our lightweight motor bikes for I recognised our code number on the mudguard.

I have enough food for a good binge today but am going to make it last several days so I can hang out until Saturday giving Monty a fortnight extra to get here. It was lovely to wake up this morning and have a buttered tea cracker, just like having breakfast in bed at home except that then I had an egg or bacon and toast and marmalade with a cup of tea. Such happy memories of married life! I have passed best part of today reading Signal the Dutch equivalent of Picture Post.

I was very lucky for water last night and have enough in a pail to fill six water bottles, which will last me easily until Sunday when I mean to move. I am lucky not to have any slates missing from my corner of the roof so that I do not get wet at every downfall.

## Thursday 28 September 1944

I very nearly did not start this day's writing for four Jerrys walked in very unexpectedly. It was a good job I was in bed or else I should have been caught. They just looked at the wireless sets and went out. I was just thinking of going downstairs that moment myself, one has kindly brought my steel helmet back.

During the night I was so ravenously hungry that my will power gave in and I finished off the other tea crackers, but I shall still stay until Saturday. If I go to a prison camp I can't get as much food as I should like whereas with the British Forces I stand a good chance. This nervous strain of living from one moment to another is playing on my nerves. There doesn't seem to be any warmth in me even my blood seems cold. How long did Ghandi fast for?

Seems a ridiculous occupation to me, I have found two miniature Oxos and some wine, jus de pommes sans alcool. It is quite strong for my weak stomach so I shall water it down and also make more of it. I carry a copper's rubber truncheon about with me and mean to knock the living daylights out of anyone who discovers me. My nerves are all on edge and the sooner I get a good meal down me the better. I feel in a terrible physical and mental state, if those lads don't come I'll go crackers. I am determined to get back to England and not end up in a POW camp. I feel wretchedly low spirited tonight and am beginning to realise the meaning of solitude. I passed this afternoon with a child's jig-saw puzzle.

## Friday 29 September 1944

For a couple of hours before daylight there was a little shelling from quite a long way off, still I was cheered at hearing it. It seemed to be concentrated on the waterfront about 50 shells I imagine.

I have a little soup powder left for tonight and then my two small apples for stewing on Saturday. This is my menu for the next two days then, who knows? My happiest moments are just as it gets dark for I rest on my bed deep in thought. Reminiscences! My thoughts are always centred around Joan and the family. I think how lucky we are to be married so young and yet so happy together. If I turn out the angel husband I plan, nobody will recognise me.

I feel terribly shaky and weak, of course it is only the food problem. There is very little noise considering the boys can't be so far off. I don't know the range of a 25 pounder gun but it seems as if they are across the river at Nijmegen and firing at Arnhem. My breath and mouth are horrid these days even though I keep cleaning my teeth it doesn't help much. I never knew what it was to go hungry before, but I know with a vengence now!

## Saturday 30 September 1944

Once again the day started with a little shelling about another 50 rounds, other than that all is quiet. I wonder how long the actual town will take to fall? Not long I hope for I am longing for one of those tinned steak puddings issued in the Field Rations, or one of those delicious rice puddings, there is nothing in the food line I cannot fancy these days.

All I think and dream of is food! I keep thinking the chaps

may have returned to England for they were only on Sicily for about four days. It would be quite an experience hitching back to England. I keep looking with longing eyes at these two apples and am itching to eat them straight off, the more I look the smaller they seem to appear. It will be quite a job getting out of this building for Jerry has a guard on the vehicles in the yard below. I had thought of messing the engines about but with a guard that is impossible. It was a good job that Whit had a sterilizing outfit in his pack for all the water I am drinking is at least a fortnight old.

Today Jerry has actually stopped looting the warehouse opposite, after continuously doing so for five days. I shall most probably be caught if I leave here for I can't speak a word of Dutch or German and where to go or what to do, I can't decide upon.

It rained all night but has now cleared up so the lads have everything in their favour. Oh to be a CQMS or a cook in these times. All I can do is sleep to stop crying out for food. All good times come to an end. Let us hope all bad ones do as well. I keep smoking my pipe to allay hunger but all in vain. I have never smoked so much in a year as in this last week.

A beautiful big black bomb has come whizzing out of the stratosphere as I write. I only wish there were hundreds to follow, yes another and a third, the building was lifted. They are a tonic for me in this state, they seem to have a delayed action. I certainly am in a unique position. I wonder if anybody else is waiting in Arnhem for the same reason as me. I'd like a paper or book to read.

I have had my soup and washed and shaved but am in a low frame of mind. I am sorry to say I can't hang on much longer for lack of food is making me feel extremely weak. I wonder where my next meal will come from.

At times I feel I don't care what happens and at others so pleased that I have evaded capture that I could sing out with joy. If I leave here and get caught I'll get some food even though low in quantity and quality. Or shall I stay here and die of starvation, hoping?

What would you do chums as Syd Walker would say? Give

yourself over to the German in attempting to escape or die like a noble Englishman? If anybody has been in a worse predicament and pulled through I take my hat off to him.

I have just cheered myself up immensely by a little burglary and an excellent prize, a 9mm FN automatic belonging to Colonel Walraven, the President of Arnhem Police. His desk was locked but by unscrewing the hinges on the back, I lifted the lid and removed a leather holster with this perfect eight round automatic with a spare magazine in the case. It is lightweight and useful to carry around. My .38 is always ready on the shed.

### Sunday 1 October 1944

Alas, it is pouring with rain and has done so nearly all night. I am thoroughly browned off with myself but realise it is no good although I hate saying so I certainly have my doubts of ever pulling out of this place alive. I shall be the luckiest chap on earth if ever I do. Several Red Cross vans have pulled up outside with nurses so the front must be some considerable way off to have them charging around.

I had a bad start today for I could not sleep last night through pains in my stomach. This morning, after I had boiled some water to warm myself I knocked it over, so you can guess how I feel, yet not quite up to shooting myself. I was hoping the Red Cross would use downstairs as a mess and then I should get some food. I would willingly give a hand with the wounded, to pass the time of waiting. But no! war isn't like that.

The sun has come out and I feel much better, it makes all things bright and beautiful. I get such a dismal feeling to wake up in the morning to think of another day to pass with nothing to do, nothing to eat and nothing to read. Our fighters are just circling the town today and don't seem inclined to shoot up the ack ack.

Three shells fell nearby this afternoon, they may have been ack ack shells that had not exploded though. All I keep thinking of is great dinners, heaped up with roast potatoes, roast beef, Yorkshire pudding and the rest, lovely thick brown gravy etc. After that I have spells of great cheese sandwiches and ham rolls with mustard.

I wonder if my next meal will be as a prisoner? I hope not. All I am striving for is against that end. I found a pot of Zellerie Zout which I take to be celery salt, so I'll have some salt water tonight. I remember hearing of Napoleon's troops surviving on a salt diet. I have found a normally uneatable pudding downstairs, I'll look in the morning for anything free of maggots.

## Monday 2 October 1944

I am feeling quite pleased with myself for this morning I scraped all the maggots and black mould from the outside of that pudding and have left the size of a medium potato. It appears to be a mixture of potatoes and carrot in pulp form with meat sauce for colouring and flavouring. I have delicately split it in two so as to have something for two days, put it in a pudding cloth and am boiling for a minute or so to kill any insects I may have missed, for there were thousands crawling all over it.

There was no shelling or bombing during the night but the fighters are having a good time around here. All I can say about the presumed advancing armies is that the Italians could have done just as well.

I am a little bothered over my water situation but I'll deal with that when it arises. Nobody on earth who isn't starving could have scraped that pudding this morning. I cannot boil it for long as I only have one cooker tablet left and it must last as long as possible.

The sun is shining and I feel quite cheerful, no doubt I'll be the opposite tomorrow for I seem to be up and down in spirits regularly.

If I am taken Prisoner of War I shall regard my whole life as wasted. I should be finishing my apprenticeship by rights, instead of idling time here.

My pudding did not come up to expectation for they had not used any flavouring in the preparing of it, so I had to use a little of my precious salt.

Just as I was writing some Jerrys came up to have a nose around but as I was sitting on my bed I had no need to move, only to lie flat and quiet.

I passed this afternoon making some holes in the Police President's black leather belt, it was too big for my now very small waist. I wonder how my Provost pals find the POW camps, it is a fortnight since they went.

**Tuesday 3 October 1944**

Throughout the night it poured with rain and I was so perished with the cold, that sleep was impossible, so once again I feel very miserable. I even thought of giving in at one moment, for it seems that I shall never be relieved. I have been in solitary confinement for 14 days now and it is enough to put the strongest minded person inside Colney Hatch.

I always thought red sky at night was shepherd's delight, but apparently that doesn't follow in Holland, for last evening was a glorious sunset. Jerry has even stooped so low as to take the carpet from downstairs.

If the electricity was on perhaps I could get one of these wireless sets working – discovered half an hour ago. I was downstairs looking out a lady's coat to wear extra for warmth when I heard footsteps come from below quite suddenly, having no time to retreat to my attic I hid behind the door of the farthest room, but I was seen, I was wearing a civilian cap and jump smock at the time, so the people did not know whether I was a German soldier or civilian not wishing to be seen. I whipped my automatic out and waited.

They turned out to be police officers, one came forward to inspect, saw me waving an automatic at him exclaimed Britisher, and together they went down the stairs faster than I went up to my shed, which was some going. I could have shot them both as easy as I could eat a good dinner now, but it isn't in my blood to kill in cold blood so I just let them go.

They did not attempt to get their own automatics out. I am now waiting for the search to begin for it seems as though a motorised company has pulled up outside according to the number of vehicles outside. I have drunk all but an inch of my wine so that Jerry will not have it, and scattered all my valuables and paybook so he'll get nothing from me.

I had just found a Bible in Dutch downstairs when I was discovered. I hope they think one Britisher isn't worth looking for. The cars have started up again and thank God I am still free. Monty will rise in my estimation when he takes this town.

### Wednesday 4 October 1944

This morning there was a beautiful sunrise, a crimson with a satin blue background, and small white pillowy puffs of cloud dotted here and there, truly a marvellous sight. I shall lie low today for I expect the building will be watched pretty closely.

I am pleased to say there was a little shelling before daylight, and the ack ack has been most intense all day, I only hope this is the beginning of the end. I never expected to have hung out so long as this. I really expected to either be shot or free by now. I would much rather Jerry blow this building up than say Kameradie for him.

I am amazed at two fully grown men being scared of a youth not come of age, yet it must have been my newly grown moustache that scared them yesterday. I wonder if we are going to cross the river higher up for all the firing is westwards from here.

As for food I am just smoking my pipe and that must do. I have the happy feeling that help isn't far off from all the ack ack is being shot up by the fighters and they seem to be paying special attention here tonight.

Passing of time is my main worry so I think I'll do some gun cleaning today. I had just finished washing when up strolled six Jerry officers. I don't think I'd bother being caught if I were single, but as I am married I have somebody else to think of. The Dutch clock I now have, seems to tick much louder when anybody is up here.

I wonder if I shall ever have to leave and ask Dutch people for assistance? I hope not for they seem ok when the British are in possession and now we have gone they are still on good terms with Jerry. Helping them with the Red Cross and supplying them with horses and carts.

Once again my stomach is calling out for food but it will have to call before I voluntarily eat POW rations. I shall have my evening meal of hot salt water, the first for three days and then some more deep thinking waiting for the darkness.

### Thursday 5 October 1944

Throughout the night and today things have relapsed into silence; at one time this morning about three dozen Fortresses flew over but that is all. It gives me confidence to see our air superiority. I am getting very unsteady on my feet and feel dizzy when I look up into the sky and brightness.

I spent the afternoon cleaning up a filthy half of a mess tin and hope to be having a British meal out of it in a few days. I reckon I now weigh six stone instead of ten, I am like a walking skeleton in fact. I must be very careful with my water for I only have one and a half water bottles left and that must last me until they come. Tomorrow is Friday, Good Friday for me I hope, for I reckon I deserve to be relieved after waiting so patiently. I shall have some hot water and so to bed.

The U.S. airforce came at midday, they were silver specks in the sky and dropped blockbusters to destroy the bridge.

### Friday 6 October 1944

Friday brings a sunny day for a change and with it four beautiful bombs at mid-day, once again on the waterfront. I made myself a holster from a piece of blanket and two boot laces, not very elegant, but it passed the time away quickly.

I have decided when I have to leave to go south towards Nijmegen, but how to cross the Rhine is my difficulty. I know the railway bridge is blown but perhaps I can manage to scramble across it somehow. I am in quite good spirits today considering my position, and hope tomorrow will bring the lads.

I am badly in need of a bath and like to get my trousers off, for they have been on nearly three weeks now. Tomorrow is my 20th day away from the Battalion and I really feel too weak to walk any distance. I retire tonight just hoping something will turn up.

## Saturday 7 October 1944

I must try and get into the lavatory on the next floor somehow, the door is locked so there must still be water in the cistern. Jerry only put bullet holes in that door, it was one he did not try to break down. Today my spirits are low again for I realise to try and cross the river is sheer madness for sentries will be posted everywhere and after that is the difficulty of crossing nomansland somewhere.

I tried imagining eating a ham sandwich this morning but to no avail. I successfully ate a candle but it was tasteless. I am in a quandary whether to go tomorrow while I am still strong enough or wait here hoping. It all depends on how much water I get tonight.

I am reckoning on leaving in the end for surely three weeks of starvation is enough to get anybody down, each day I become weaker and my faith diminishes. I should not think 64 miles in three weeks is hardship for our army.

## Sunday 8 October 1944

This morning at 6am I managed to get a jug of water, enough for three water bottles. It came from a filthy sink that was stopped up and I scooped it out finding nothing else. I found an oil lamp which I shall convert into a burner for my hot water.

Today is a typical winter's Sunday morning, a very low mist making everything dark and damp and everything is deathly quiet, that takes me back to my camping days. I have neither heard nor seen an aircraft this last two days or a gun since yesterday. I have given up expecting the troops now and shall just hang on until this water runs out for it is definitely the last here. My thoughts are still full of food and when I get to a NAAFI I'll automatically order double rations.

### Monday 9 October 1944

Things are coming to a pitch for once again it is very overcast and miserable so much so that I considered shooting myself at one time. I saw a Jerry tank in close up for the first time this morning, it doesn't look as good as ours. At one time I lay on my shed writhing in agony with pains in my stomach. I screwed myself into a little ball and cried out.

Once again things are very quiet, we may be back at Cherbourg for all I know. I have my doubts as to whether an Englishman will ever read this narrative of my plight. It is nearly dark and I have had a cup of hot water. A couple of shells have just whizzed over so that cheers me.

### Tuesday 10 October 1944

Shells came throughout the night which kept me awake but that didn't worry me, I was glad to hear it. This morning it started raining, and has done so all day without a stop, so of course visibility being nil, nothing else has happened.

I have been reading this account of my adventures through today and am very glad I started to keep a diary, for otherwise I should not know what day it was.

Tuesday is definitely my hoodoo day for I was having a quiet pipe when up strolled some more Jerries very quietly. This afternoon I went through all the lunch bags I could find downstairs for crumbs and found two large ones which I thoroughly enjoyed. I wonder where it will all end?

### Wednesday 11 October 1944

It rained during the night once again but there was a little shelling which greatly cheered me. I am extremely light on my water, going without on alternate days, for there is no more about. When it is gone I must ask the assistance of the Dutch people or be taken Prisoner of War. Visibility is still bad but it may clear up later in the day.

At long last the rain has stopped. I brought another two blankets up from downstairs so that I may keep warm in my last few days of freedom.

There is just a little ack ack in the distance but no sign of artillery or bombing in this locality. I reckon on making my water last until Friday but I don't expect the lads to get here by then.

I reckon to go just after midnight one night with a shell dressing wrapped around each boot and attempt to cross the river on the back of a lorry going over the bridge or crawl across the railway bridge. I don't even know if there are civilians in that direction, they may have been cleared out by Jerry.

I may find a young couple that are National Socialist and all for Hitler and his cronies, there is one consoling factor, I'll either get food or be shot and not want any. I am far from confident of ever getting out of town!

My spirits are quite high for the fighters are flying around but haven't dropped anything so far. I spent this morning cutting out beautiful pictures of the continent mostly Holland from some handbooks, and this afternoon by sorting out some Dutch stamps. I am making things as pleasant as possible for my last couple of days.

## Thursday 12 October 1944

I am extremely pleased with myself for as it became dusk yesterday I went downstairs looking for tobacco and found a box of 19 cigars. A bomb fell at 5pm yesterday and about eight during the night, there was a lot of air activity and heavy shelling.

Early this morning on my expeditions, I had a wonderful discovery, a slice of bread and a shop ginger cake, it was very mildewy but I haven't let that worry me. I also found a Reich banknote of 10000 marks whether it has any value I don't know. In one drawer I found another pipe so I am in high spirits, even some more tobacco.

If only I can find some water I'll hang on until the lads come. The coppers came in today the first time for about a fortnight. I am down to my last water bottle so must do something about it in the morning.

### Friday 13 October 1944

Friday the 13th. Strange but true! I was unlucky this morning for after making a beautiful job of making a key for the President's latrine door, I actually accidently flushed the cistern from inside, was I mad, I could hardly believe it for the moment, so the water situation is more acute than expected.

I had a delicious breakfast of two slices of cake boiled for a minute in a kettle. It boiled into one mass but was very tasty. I'll do some more tonight for I am so hungry. At the weekend it is a month since we left England. There was no shelling or bombing last night.

I have busied myself cutting out magazine pictures of Germans today. I must find some water. I'll have another attempt in the morning for some. Ack ack was heavy today and two bombs fell. I could easily finish the cake up but must save some for tomorrow.

### Saturday 14 October 1944

I was up at sunrise this morning in my quest for water, but proved unsuccessful. I have come to the conclusion that there isn't a water tank in the building, it must be straight off the main.

I went through some of the coppers' lockers and managed to find three rusks, some apples and some sugar so will be stewing apples tonight in a small amount of water.

Unluckily I was seen by a patrol while on the ground floor this morning and had to get upstairs in double quick time before I was recognised as the Britisher of a fortnight ago. The apples turned out beautifully sweet and tasty, I used all the sugar on them.

## Sunday 15 October 1944

I heralded my fourth week in Holland by being up and on the prowl an hour before it was light. For the locker room is on the ground floor and faces the road and I did not wish to be seen there, also I had to make some considerable noise opening metal lockers. I was not so lucky as I had hoped but nevertheless was quite successful.

Some dried milk, some cocoa blocks and some sugar made me a type of sweet gruel or custard this morning, and two soft tomatoes I placed in hot water to fill them out I had at mid-day.

I have had quite a restful day sorting out pictures once again. I have lived for a month now spending nothing and yet having a month's credit, but I feel older in myself and certainly looked it, after I had shaved this morning.

Life is so hectic I shall not know myself once things get back to normal. I found a kettle of water this morning and by having waterless days I reckon to hang on until Saturday next when surely they'll be through. I am fed up with my own company at this moment and yet at times I feel quite confident all will be well and at other times things seem so black, I feel like throwing the towel in.

What a unique position. I may become a Prisoner of War anytime I so desire, on the other hand I may become one without wanting. I have certainly taken to pipe smoking through this period and don't suppose I shall ever give it up now.

This morning I equipped myself with a pack of cards, some mittens and a scarf. I think I have had the luck of the devil himself to have lasted so long in a town over-ridden with Germans. My night starts at 6.30pm when it is dark and reveille is at 5.30am so I don't do too badly for sleep. I am worried over Joan for she has no idea where or how I am, one good point of being a Prisoner of War is that I could send a letter home.

## Monday 16 October 1944

Today has been quite eventful for I was up at daybreak and found some more lockers. They all had padlocks and so I did some housebreaking. Two pears, more cocoa blocks and salt and pepper was this morning's find with a packet of coffee. So this evening I had two spoonfuls of salt, one of pepper and one of ground coffee, boiled up together it has made my eyes and nose run. Jerry has disturbed me twice already today.

It has rained a little today and things have been rather quiet. My water problem was solved by collecting the rain water in pots and jam jars under the holes in the roof so now I have plenty for the present. I am just beginning to get used to this hermits life and pass the time by doing odd jobs at special times, sorting out pictures is the main one.

I have been cut off from the outside world a month now and have no idea how the war is progressing.

### Tuesday 17 October 1944

I found nothing in the food line this morning but came across a lot of prisoners articles which have yielded many an interest for me. They date back to about 1920 so I presume they are not claimed.

I have found a large sheath knife, a wrist watch and a rosary. Also some Dutch money to spend once I leave here. I have equipped myself with a pair of slippers so may leave the blankets off my boots at last.

Jerry has been up once again this afternoon but after a month on my own I now feel confident the troops will get here sometime.

### Wednesday 18 October 1944

I am still in quite high spirits for this morning on my daily rounds I found a l lb. pot of pickled whelks and cockles with 'bewaren 1 October 1944' on the label, so I am only 18 days late. Tonight I shall have a third, with plenty of salt and pepper added for my daily meal.

Things are very quiet once again for it has poured with rain nearly all day but nevertheless I feel quite pleased with myself for I now have a full kit of house-breaking tools including a one and a half inch chisel.

### Thursday 19 October 1944

This morning I had the luck of the devil for I burst open a

locker with a large number of onions in, so today I have occupied eating and trying to pickle onions with the whelks. I wished I could find something to take them down for a raw onion needs bread, but to my extra empty stomach it tastes excellent. With the onions I found a box of salt.

I am exceedingly thin, my stomach is flat from hip bone to hip bone and my usual footballers knees far from it. It is still very quiet outside and it would not surprise me to hear we were back in Brussels, as I dreamt Dad told me. I hope I don't do much walking once I leave here, I am not fit, my left hip is numb. It has rained a lot today but my spirits are still high.

### Friday 20 October 1944

I now have enough food to last for a fortnight in the shape of half a sack of onions which I fetched up this morning, and on an average of three per day I can last out. I am anxiously waiting for it to rain again for some more water.

I was extremely lucky in finding four biscuits, some sweets that had gone to sugar on the floor and some tea cubes, all of which the mice had nibbled but in these times it takes more than that to turn me off food. I had never risked crossing the back yard before for the gate is on the main road.

From a Gammon Bomb I took the plastic explosive and will use it for brewing up. I found an armourer's shop up in the attic and now have a 4.5mm air rifle. So altogether I am very pleased with myself. All I want now is to meet the lads.

I went to the lavatory last night the first time for a month. It must be the onions!

### Saturday 21 October 1944

This morning I had a change from onions for breakfast, for finding a biscuit tin with a handful of crumbs in and some treacle from a locker, I mixed them together and made a porridge. I hope the lads do strike for Arnhem eventually for I should hate to be taken a POW now after hiding for so long. There has not been the usual ack ack fire for the last three days.

Tomorrow completes my fifth week in Holland, and I reckon I have done quite well considering the circumstances.

My day is now a very busy one, it starts at 4.45am with my house-breaking kit to open any lockers before light at 6.30. I search until about 8am when Jerry is wide awake and then I start with my fire boiling onions.

The time until 9.30 passes very quickly and then I sit down on my bed sorting out the various oddments I have collected from the lockers. This I make last until 4pm when I wash and heat my evening drink of salt water or tea for tonight, the first I have tasted for over a month. During the night I eat raw onions with salt and make my eyes and nose run no end.

I wonder how I'll be this time next week, fed up with onions no doubt, but they have opened my bowels and that is a relief.

My thoughts are always of Joan and how she must be worrying but I hope like me she has faith that all will be well in the end. Mum and Dad must be regretting me joining the suicide squad, as somebody kindly remarked to Mum when wearing my cap badge in her coat.

### Sunday 22 October 1944

I slept with very depressing thoughts last night for I put an onion in a mess tin and heated it, of course in five minutes it was not cooked just hard and hot and that was my supper yesterday; after eating half I was very sick so decided a monotonous diet of raw onions was no good for me. I then decided I must take the risk of getting into the Victoria Hotel and see if any food was left, so in the early hours (4.15am) I sallied forth. I now have porridge, flour and seasoning to take the onions down with so I am very satisfied with myself. I am using cigar boxes to make fire with and spent until 10am cooking this morning. I am hoping for more rain.

### Monday 23 October 1944

Today has been most depressing for while trying to sort out some drinks in the hotel, I took in a mouthful of ammonia, it immediately took all the lining from my mouth and tongue

No. **3|AAC|1|2.**
(If replying, please quote above No.)

Army Form B. 104—83

S̶I̶R̶ O̶R̶ MADAM,

I regret to have to inform you that a report has been received from the War Office to the effect that (No.) 14363066 (Rank) Private (Name) PEATLING Robert William (Regiment) ARMY AIR CORPS.

was posted as " missing " on the 25th September 1944 in North West Europe

The report that he is missing does not necessarily mean that he has been killed, as he may be a prisoner of war or temporarily separated from his regiment.

Official reports that men are prisoners of war take some time to reach this country, and if he has been captured by the enemy it is probable that unofficial news will reach you first. In that case I am to ask you to forward any postcard or letter received at once to this Office, and it will be returned to you as soon as possible.

Should any further official information be received it will be at once communicated to you.

I am,

S̶I̶R̶ O̶R̶ MADAM,

Your obedient Servant,

Officer in charge of Records.

**IMPORTANT.**

Any change of your address should be immediately notified to this Office.

Wt. 30051/1249 400,000 (16) 9/39 KJL/8812 Gp 698/3 Forms/B.104—83/9 and brought blood. I felt terrible and did not care at that time whether I showed a light or made a noise; the state I was in I could have killed any Jerries that discovered me with a madman's strength, this was at 5am this morning.

So now I cannot smoke or eat, for my mouth and tongue is so tender and as for eating onions with salt – well! I made a limp macaroni pudding with dried milk and added baking powder instead of flour to thicken it, so that wasn't nice.

I found some very sweet lemonade so that will save a little water. There is very little noise these days, one wouldn't know there was a war on.

### Tuesday 24 October 1944

I overslept this morning until 6am too late to go into the restaurant for it is light and I cannot risk it. I have had quite a busy day most of it working out recipes especially of spices for the onions. I nearly have the recipe for bread worked out if only I had the necessary heat to cook it.

There is very little air activity and I am beginning to think that the troops may never get here, but I shall hang on for as long as it is humanly possible. I have plenty of food now and two jugs of water from the water softener next door.

I must get some more cigar boxes for firewood and if I have time will go over the place thoroughly in the morning. I hope to make reveille at 3am and at 6am start preparing my onions and milk pudding.

### Wednesday 25 October 1944

The cooking today has been excellent, some thick porridge this morning at 8am and then some well cooked onions. Tonight I had some custard. The cake I made was a little underdone, it started off as bread then I added sugar and made it a steamed pudding. Afterwards I changed my mind, added a cereal that looks like bread crumbs and ate it with some jam. I have enough water for three or four days at this rate of cooking.

I was up very early this morning and am a little headachy so will retire early tonight. Something is wrong with my left thigh for there is no feeling in the muscle, it is cold and numb. There is still no ack ack so I wonder if ever they will come here and free me.

### Thursday 26 October 1944

I have had quite an interesting day since my 4am reveille, for I found a considerable amount of 10,000 Mark notes under the bed of the proprietor. It was scattered about the room for Jerry had already looted everywhere, so I expect it is valueless, otherwise I am a millionaire. The ack ack fire in the distance has brightened up. Jerry hasn't been around this building much today.

But just as I am about to light my fire he has come in and I am scared to light up because of the smoke and smell I make up here. 5pm I have just eaten some delicious stewed onions with plenty of flavouring and they were delicious.

I now have a thick cocoa flavoured macaroni pudding. Then a long smoke of one of my numerous pipes and so to bed at 5.30. The cake I have made is for during the night as every two hours regularly I wake up, I am a very light sleeper these days.

Tomorrow I hope for a 4am reveille and then I'll try another shop. I hope for some potatoes for they would help the monotonous onions down. I seem to have encouraged the fleas and during the night I heard mice or rats.

### Friday 27 October 1944

The next shop after the hotel turned out to be a bakers. Jerry had looted any biscuits I had hoped for but I found quite a large amount of dried fruit all ready for jam making. There was some marmalade in a pot with insects crawling over it but mixed up with the rest and heated it should kill them all. Also some apples, some black, some very soft but anyway it is all food.

I now have plenty of water and know where there is a geyser that should be full. Best of all I found grease in the form of Boter Essence so I shall mix it with my cakes when I make them. They have to be made in daily stages for I can only have a fire for about an hour each morning and then Jerry is about the yard and building.

Ref. No. **NF/m/5375**......

OFFICE FORM E – 158.

-/MMW.

Hawkhill Avenue,
Edinburgh. 7.

*23* / *10*/19*44*.

Dear Madam,

I have learned with regret that you have been informed
that  Army No. **1436 2066.**  Name *PEATLING R.W.*

Rank *PTE.*  Unit *A.A.C.*

has been reported as missing.

You will doubtless wish to know without delay your position
regarding the allowance payable to you until such time as further
information about the soldier is forthcoming.

The allowance at present being paid to you on his behalf
will be continued until **8.4.45** at **42/6** per week, subject
to any adjustment that may be necessary as a result of further
information concerning the soldier being received before the latter
date.

---

Should no news of the soldier be received by **8.4.45.**
the rate at which the allowance may be continued will be subject to
review and a further communication will be sent to you.

I am enclosing Army Form 0.1859/~~1860~~ which you should
complete and forward IMMEDIATELY to the War Office (F.4.P.W.) in the
enclosed envelope.  It is essential that you supply the required
information AT ONCE as delay in doing so may result in your being
without any allowance while the subsequent rate is being determined.

I am, Madam,
Your obedient Servant,

To: *Mrs. J. Peatling.*
...............

*a.b.Ray*
*Lieut.*
Regimental Paymaster.

55

On that fire I cook onions, porridge and my hot drink. I have a marvellous arrangement of tins for doing it. The tins at the side are for my drink and onions, at the bottom is a cigarette tin with the makings of a cake in and on top is the porridge, after 20 minutes when my porridge is cooked I put another saucepan of onions on for about an hour's cooking.

Sometimes there is another form of cake or pudding being steamed on top of the porridge. I am getting plenty of cooking experience.

Just as I came out of the bakers this morning two Jerry convoys passed, one in either direction, one stopped a little way up the road and I thought my adventures would finish this morning especially if they had disembarked for a break. It was then 5.45 and I had left it rather late in getting back as I had such a lot of tins to sort out. The day is very cloudy and I can feel the November weather closing in. I often wonder if my boys are still in the line, I hope they are back in England by now for that is where I hope to go after leaving here and I think I deserve to as well.

Jerry has not been up here at all today and I have had a good day cooking. I am longing for the day when food is no longer my worry. I have everything a chap could wish for except freedom, anyhow I have more than in a POW camp. Another pay-day I have missed, I'll be quite rich soon.

## Saturday 28 October 1944

Today has seen the completion of my 40 days and 40 nights banishment to the wilderness. It has been quite pleasant,

I overslept until 5am this morning despite my early retirement last night. It was a good job that I left my evening meal until later today for Jerry came up for the second time this afternoon when I should have been in the middle of a cloud of smoke. Something representing bread and onions is my meal tonight, it has been boiled and now has to be fried. Afterwards I have a milk pudding with apple, lemon, fruit and vanilla flavouring, all oddments I have found from the bakers. I hope I don't get any visitors while the cooking is in progress.

Ack ack was on an increased scale today but there is no sign of any troop movement in the town. I have food and water but am pining to see our troops.

I always have a couple of small meals during the long night, either one of the best of the mouldy apples or an onion. I have had my fair share of onions for the duration.

## Sunday 29 October 1944

It was six weeks ago about this time that I had a safe landing in Holland. I thought my worries were over for good at having such a soft landing and a marvellous welcome from the people, but it appears that my worries were about to start.

The time has seemed to pass very quickly for every day since writing this diary I have been busy occupying my mind. I found what I have always looked for this morning, potatoes and pounds of them, so I had my first potato this morning for breakfast, and hope to have a proper dinner of potatoes and onions on a plate about 4pm today.

Jerry did not come into work today, but two parties of troops have been up looking for loot. They are rather late, their predecessors have had all the decent wireless sets. I now have two English books, one on Wireless and the other The Invasion of 1910 by William Le Queux, published in 1906. But I haven't time to read them for preparing my meals and cutting up firewood takes all my time. It is really getting typical November weather, cold and wet!

Ack ack is still in the distance. My food store has now turned into a regular larder so I have nothing to grumble at in that respect. All I want is a bath, a haircut and the troops then I shall regard myself as the luckiest chap in Holland.

## Monday 30 October 1944

It has turned out extremely cold today, and I very nearly had to break the ice on my washing water. My food problems are all settled and with the knowledge of a store of water I am well away. For breakfast this morning I ate so much that I had to sleep from 11am until 2pm to let it go down. I hope over-eating is not very bad for me. I have another dinner cooked for 4pm, it just needs heating again.

Aircraft activity is once again nil, due to the very high wind I expect, for slates are being blown off roofs quite a lot. If I were single I should really enjoy this life of adventure, but the thought of Joan, Mum and Dad worrying over me takes all thoughts of the excitement away. For in those three I now realise I have the three best friends anyone could have. I hope I can be worthy of them all and treat them in the correct capacity once I return.

Tomorrow sees the end of October, I hope I don't have to see the end of November out in this place, although I reckon that I can do it with food and rain alternate days. Jerry was late in coming this morning so I am hoping the front isn't receding and they are moving up with it.

The town is nearly deserted, only occasionally do I see anyone now, but it only wants one person to challenge me and the game is up.

A specimen of the money I found scattered under a
bed in the Victoria Hotel. I thought I had found Eldorado
but have since been informed of its value!
It is dated 1922 when Germany suffered an enormous
inflationary period and money was worthless.

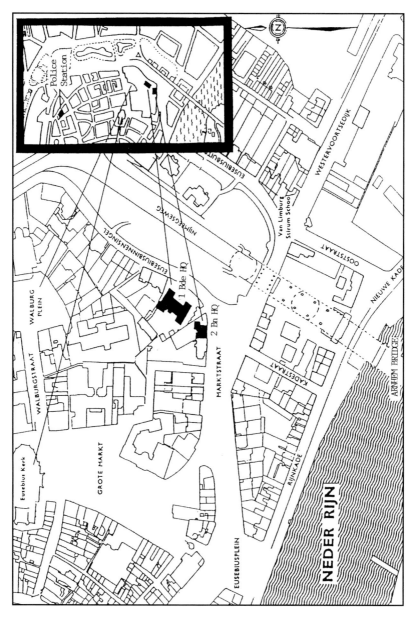

Arnhem Bridge showing (inset) the proximity
of the main police station.

*Map from The Pegasus Patrol*

# CHAPTER THREE

# Tuesday 31 October 1944

*Meet wonderful, brave, jovial Dutch Underground
army lads of my own age, teach them weapon cleaning,
a little English and how not to handle explosives.*

I NOW find that I am getting miserable with myself for
very few people or vehicles pass to look at, the coppers are
in and I am suffering from indigestion through over-eating.
It is very misty and there has not been any ack ack fire all the
morning. The day started unusually for I arose at 2.30am as
I only had some wooden boxes to collect from the Bakers
for firewood. I thought if I collected them I could sleep
until 6.30am instead of arising about 4.30am before Jerry is
about for them.

I had potatoes once again for breakfast and some stewed
apples. I am quite proud of my cooking these days. But as for
hopes of the British Forces – well they sink lower and lower
each day, like my faith in Monty.

In fact I am in the state that I don't care what happens so
long as I let the folks at home know that I am not
dead as they must surely be thinking by now. I keep
wondering how and when it will all end for it surely must
one day. I have the confidence in our troops to come here
and now it is up to other people to fulfil them.

Last night I had a most horrible feeling inside me and had
to get up for an hour to let my food digest. I am afraid I shall
have to use the cigars I was saving as my tobacco is finished.

Tuesday usually brings something exciting but up to the
present it is very misty and dull, but it is early yet – half-an-
hour later the police came up, just as I had finished writing
and after looking about one climbed up onto the beams to

look out of the skylight for I had left the top off since the early days here, he casually looked around and of course noticed all the tins of food on the opposite shed. He called to the other two; another policeman and a woman and they inspected my food. They then crossed to my smaller shed and I kept perfectly still hoping to pass unnoticed in the darkness. One stepped across and took my .38 revolver from the end of the shed.

I thought I had not been discovered but ten minutes later the policemen came up again. I rose to meet them with my automatic and they backed away but I showed them my paper with 'Can you hide me' etc., on it and one said he could not as he was a National Socialist, the other a Second Lieutenant was in favour of the British, so after a lot of broken English with gabbling in Dutch to each other the First Lieutenant said he would not tell Jerry so long as I did not spy.

I gave him my word and they gave me the news that Nijmegen was in British hands ten miles away; that of the 10,000 paratroops dropped here in September 6,500 are POWs and 3,500 are dead, so it looks as if I am the only survivor so far from our Battalion. They told me that only one of the lads in the police building was shot, it was Sergeant Callaway, the rest are POWs: were they lucky?

One has promised to come back but the National Socialist said he could not. They gave me a cigarette and I gave them each a 5 Mark and a 2.5 Guilder note, British issue. They promised to keep it quiet and only wanted them for a souvenir. So Tuesday has turned out exciting after all.

It appears that the troops have been in the same position for about a month, that King George has been to Nijmegen and that General Dempsey has been sent back to America for reasons quite obvious. I am very pleased with the news the first for six weeks. They also told me that the town is evacuated of all civilians except for a few essential workers; the bridge is no more and the only way to cross is swim or boat. They were surprised when I said I was only 20 for I have not shaved my upper lip since leaving England and now have a moustache, which must make me look older.

It is now 3.30pm and since 1.30pm I have been a civvie and no longer at my old address, it all happened in a flash. The Second Lieutenant came back and said he did not trust the other officer and that he was in touch with the Underground movement and had arranged for a civilian to come and take me home.

Johannes Penseel arrived at the attic door alone, with a suitcase containing a suit, he tapped out the V for Victory sign on the door and called out,'Are you there mine friend?'. I did not answer and left him to call again, he did and we met.He waited while I shaved and then we went down to the street to see the policeman waiting on the corner with his bicycle ready to escort me to the shop in Velperplein. I was changed into civvies, packed my washing kit, tobacco and revolver and was on my way.

After a five minute walk, I found myself on the second floor of a large house on the top floor above a shop. I am going to hide in a well looted bedroom with a 30 inch trap door in the floor, it leads to a ten foot long passage, five feet deep but only 18 inches across.

I am in contact with a Dutch Army chap John, who hid from the Gestapo for 18 months in this hole, he is 25 and thought that I was 27, so it must have aged me living in that police building.

As soon as I arrived there was a large saucepan of hot potatoes and greens mashed for my dinner. I gorged it all readily and once again had the belly ache. John speaks very good English, he said forward elements are in Elst, four miles away. His mother can feed me for they are living two doors away in the Nederland Bank for they have a shelter there and use it for sleeping. I certainly have had an exciting Tuesday and am now waiting for my tea meal to be brought. Then I shall be off for twelve hours solid sleep. I actually sat on a lavatory seat instead of perching over a Signal magazine. I shall now have nothing to do all day but write and read the 'Pawns Count' by Philip Oppenheim he has provided. It looks as though I have lost my Sir Robert Baden-Powell and Kipling's 'Kim' for they were in Mr Ainslie's kit.

Poor old Jock Dunlop and Harry Back had only been

married about a week. What an exciting end of October. It is now 7pm and I am down in my hole reading by an oil lamp. I really don't fancy the tight squeeze on my sides but otherwise am very comfortable with the spread from a settee and a thick blanket.

At 5pm John brought his younger brother of 21 along (Marinus but prefers Martin) with some very weak sweet tea (no milk) and some minty sweets.

Then at 6pm came tea proper, three fried eggs and numerous pieces of bread and butter with cheese and something like luncheon meat on. Also two slices of black bread with sugar on it tasted like cake-cum-bread-pud, and two large apples for later on, so I am well away in the food line.

We have a code word as he comes into the building, he whistles a song the 'Zuider Zee' so that I know all is well. I must thank these people for the risk they are taking in looking after me, they are allowed in Arnhem for technical reasons but it is a blind for the Underground.

John says breakfast at 9am in the morning, so I'll be able to sleep late and not have to bother about any more early morning prowling. I am sure Tuesday will be the day the troops will come, for Tuesday has been my lucky day throughout this escapade.

Chapter two had a sudden ending and closed without me giving it a second thought. I was so pleased to have left it behind. Now comes the realisation that I am behind enemy lines in civilian clothes.

During the summer of 1944 on a Sunday morning, we were assembled at the cinema Grantham to be told how to behave, if captured, by two Officers who had been in that position fairly recently. We were aware of only giving your name, rank and number to the enemy and the reasons, but there were now some additions for us.

They were: If captured, escape at first opportunity, before you have been interrogated or documented. Front line troops have no interest in you but once you are passed back, you are of interest to the Intelligence interviewer, and will be guarded closely.

If you escape you are of great nuisance value to the enemy.

On your return we want to know, who, what, where and when? You are invaluable to us. If you should change into civilian clothes, you are at risk of being shot.

We were each provided with a short hacksaw blade, a finger nail size compass and certain members, (me included being a signaller), with a silk map of Europe.

## Wednesday 1 November 1944

I have been chilly all day even though I have a shirt, two pullovers and a waistcoat and top coat on. Once again I have done extremely well for food. Six slices of bread and jam with a bottle of tea for breakfast, some excellent coffee at 11am and another great panful of vegetables at 1.30. It was really twice as much as I needed but I ate it for I hate saying it is too much; for sweet was a blancmange of toffee flavour. Very tasty indeed.

Since then I have had some afternoon tea, some cake and some sweets. John has provided me with a box of food in case there is street fighting and I cannot be reached. It included pre-war biscuits, a tin of milk, sardines, apples and peas and some concentrated bread in biscuit form.

Time seems to hang waiting for them to come and talk to me. I slept well last night, there is just room for me to lie flat in my hideaway. I asked for some tobacco and some was provided at the next visit. According to John who listens to a wireless set stored away unknown to the Germans, Mr Churchill has been to see Stalin in Moscow.

We have quite a good bridgehead over the Waal at Nijmegen, so should be striking for a bridge head at Arnhem soon. Artillery is still in the distance although I imagined there would be more noise for an army not so far off.

My second phase here has given me complete confidence for I now have someone to talk to. A friend of John's went to the police building for my clock yesterday.

## Thursday 2 November 1944

I had an extremely good nights sleep last night after a good tea, five slices of bread and a plate of scrambled eggs. I then had two slices with luncheon meat and four with cheese for my evening meal.

I read my book until 7.15pm by my oil lamp and then slept until 10pm when nature called and I ate the bread and cheese, a piece of cake and some sweets.

Then I retired until 3am when I had two apples and the luncheon meat. I have an enormous appetite these days, even though I get very little exercise – making up for my six weeks of starvation I suppose.

This morning I slept until the 'V' sign tapped on my trap door awakened me for porridge at 9.15am. The pan I have for my dinner is, I imagine, an enamel potato tureen, suitable for three or four persons so you can guess how I am overeating.

It is quite a well-to-do family looking after me, mother, father and two sons. They have a young girl of six years living with them, Elizabeth. She is a Jewess whose parents have been taken away to Poland so they have unofficially adopted her. They lived in this house, above the shop which belongs to them, they sell all electrical equipment, Hoover and lamp stands etc. Jerry broke into every room breaking the doors down and stealing everything he fancied.

All the cupboards were let in the walls and now the doors are hanging off their hinges, contents of drawers strewn over the floor and everything messed up, it is a large house on four floors and a basement, each of four rooms.

The news with my breakfast was that troops landed at Flushing yesterday morning so we now have a direct sea route with Holland. I hope they are unloading bridge building equipment for crossing the Rhine at Arnhem. I am going to fix up a pyjama coat on the window so that John can see it as he comes in and if all isn't well inside I take it down and he keeps away, this is to stop Jerry catching him bringing me food.

During the night there was plenty of artillery fire but I reckon it will be at least a week before they reach the river bank, there should be plenty of air activity before then. John tells me that the airborne situation is better than the German report that the police gave me.

The Yanks at Nijmegen hung on and some of the British

Forces met up with them so my Battalion may still be intact. I am still hoping to go straight to England. John is hoping to go as well and train for the Dutch Army and free the Dutch East Indies from the Japs.

Every month they have to beg for a new passport to stay in the town from Jerry. There are many fresh infantry troops coming into the town so perhaps they are expecting a big push here. Jerry has taken all the male personnel for digging trenches west of the town so we have decided the bridge-head will be in between Wagenengen and Arnhem, that will be about Heelsum where I landed on September 17th.

My new 'father' is something of an electrical fiend for there are lamps everywhere: on the walls, tables, piano and even an owl's eyes light up in an ornament. I have two very good friends in these brothers' of mine and only hope I can come back and see their beautiful town in peace time with Joan.

These people are looking after me better than I could expect from my own countrymen. I have had my morning coffee and cake, the coffee was beautifully milky and sweet, the best I have ever tasted. John has shown me how to get out of the house by the back way and cross to the bank where they are all living in case of an emergency: if Jerry sets fire to the house etc. He has just brought me in the nicest and thickest set of underclothes I have ever seen just like smooth fur and new, easily worth a guinea a piece.

I left England in warm weather so did not wear winter underclothes, but should have had them from my kit-bag by now. John is trying to get a letter through to Joan through the Red Cross, I hope it is successful even if it means going through Geneva and round the world.

It is now 4pm and since 1.30 have been flat on my back in pain, for the dinner of potatoes, carrots and onions all mixed up with a delicately braised piece of steak, about four inches square, it was the first piece of meat in seven weeks, it proved too much for me in one go. I had three attempts at it, finishing up with a plate of apples. I also have a dozen apples for my reserve stock and a jar of sugar to sweeten anything I wish.

I felt compelled to write a note of thanks to my new

'mother' today for it is no small job feeding my appetite in these times. The Germans use all the Dutch food whenever possible, leaving very little for them. German lorries are loading up with furniture and bedding from the evacuated houses and carted off to Germany for the bombed out cities. I have given my last 2.5 guilder note to John with my paper, Can you hide me etc., as a souvenir. It seems strange not having any food or house-breaking worries.

### Friday 3 November 1944

It was seven weeks ago today that I last had a bath and this morning John brought me a pail of water nearly boiling so I had a stand up bath, I certainly needed it. I had some more porridge for breakfast with some German bread, it isn't so dark or hard as the Dutch.

Pop openly asked Jerry for it and he gave the bread. For dinner I had pea soup with potatoes and onions and a piece of cow, very tasty indeed. I only had to make one attempt at it today, and three pancakes for sweet.

With the inhabitants of Arnhem forcibly evacuated,
German lorries with trailers came each day for carpets, lino,
bedding and furniture, making good the items lost in the
bombing of Germany. To be caught taking photographs was a
most serious crime. *Photo: de Booys Agency*

John has a passport for me of a lad that was killed by our bombing when we arrived. He resembles my features somewhat, the only trouble is I shall have to shave my tash off. I am to appear dumb if any Jerry wants to engage me in conversation.

My new mother's reply to my letter was that she worries over me like she would her son, she also sent the family photograph that I asked for and a book called 'Dear Old London', photos of London in 1920.

If only I could let Joan know I was safe and well I should be in my element here. John tells me the V1 isn't finished yet so I suppose poor ARP warden, father, is suffering on his lonesome still. I hope all is well at home. I am positive artillery fire is concentrating in this direction so things may happen soon.

Martin brought a civvie up with him who was very anxious to see the Tommy, he wanted my name as a souvenir, pressed cigarettes on me and gave me the news that a patrol had crossed the Rhine and come within five minutes distance of here, reconnoitred and retired safely. I mentioned Boy Scouts to Martin and he said he was one until Jerry made it an illegal organisation.

### Saturday 4 November 1944

It makes me shudder when I think of those six weeks without speaking to a soul or having one decent meal. I arose at 7am this morning and had a good look over downstairs, it was just like the electricity showrooms. I only wish I had been discovered by that policeman earlier, for this existence is heaven itself.

We are worried in case they use compulsory measures to evacuate the technical civilians (*me*) when the fighting starts, if so I am going with them. I hope it doesn't happen, for to be caught in civilian clothes means to be shot as a spy. POW camp doesn't enter into it. I have my revolver and with six rounds, six Jerries will come with me.

John says Jerry is very worried and annoyed at us using flame throwers for they have nothing to combat it. For the first time for a very long time my tongue is clear, and I am beginning to feel much better. It is now a month since I have had any feeling in my thigh muscle and I am very worried about it.

Tomorrow's date is always one of excitement to English lads, I wonder if they'll bring it to Arnhem this year. I now have a girl's book 'Emily of New Moon' by L. M.Montgomery.

I have had company all day today for the boys have been clearing up the next room and put a stove in for cooking if I get stranded. John and I had a talk on our post-war plans, his are to unite the Continent by politics so there will not be another war, and mine are to make Joan happy and to make up for the worrying time she must be going through.

### Sunday 5 November 1944

I arose at 8.40am this morning after a very good nights sleep, I washed and dressed just in time for breakfast. I also took my socks off to sleep for the first time so my blood must be getting thicker. The new mother came to see her adopted son this morning, she is very much the same build as my proper mother and speaks a little English.

Rumour has it that we have crossed the Rhine west of Arnhem but we wait for the British report to come in. Sixteen Jerries were found dead and are believed to have committed suicide in Arnhem.

A member of the Underground was found shot here yesterday. They tell me that the average Jerry realises that the war is lost and only a certain few of the SS still have confidence.

A very heavy artillery duel raged last night just like the old September days. Martin became a barber this morning and cut my two month old locks and made a very good job of it. For dinner there was a real English faggot of minced beef, very tasty, with a custard blancmange afterwards. I'll be as fat as Teddy Brown with this eating and sleeping in no time.

John's girlfriend known to all as 'Baby' came up this afternoon together with the little adopted one, Elizabeth. John's girl had a beautiful brown fur coat on worth 1,000 guilders (less than £100). Once again I had an egg for tea, this time boiled. I am feeding better than with the Army in England. It is extremely windy today and the gunfire still heavy.

## Monday 6 November 1944

Surely a miracle happened that I am still free in a German occupied town, I now live like a lord, being waited on hand and foot. All I do is eat good wholesome food and have plenty of sleep. I only hope the V1 menace is nearly over and that Joan is comforted in some small way that I am safe. I mean to bring her back to Arnhem to meet all my good friends at the first opportunity I have.

I took my khaki shirt off today for it was a little grubby after seven weeks and have boiled it all day on the stove. My good brothers have brought me a shirt and tie so now I am all the gentleman. Martin has given me an exquisite pipe of skull and cross-bone design, also a photograph of himself. This town has been in the front line for a long time now, but I still give it another fortnight before it falls.

## Tuesday 7 November 1944

Today is normally my hoodoo day but I hope I don't have as much excitement as last week for my heart could not stand it. My nerves are not in a very good condition for every sound during these past few weeks has meant life or death to me. As far as shelling is concerned I am bomb happy, nothing pleases me more than to hear them whizzing down for I know at the other end of them are Englishmen. We people in Arnhem are only waiting for one moment in our lives and it is all everyone talks of.

There is another moment I hope for and that is to be back in England with Joan, for she is my life partner and I mean to make her happy in my short existence.

I slept extremely well last night, asleep at 7.30pm, supper at 11pm and slept until John and Martin called me for breakfast at 9am. I rinsed my shirt out in cold water this morning and it has lost quite a bit of its colour through ten hours of boiling.

The daughter of the caretaker of the Bank came to see me

this morning, she is 18 but even though had three years of English at school, could not converse with me, for I spoke too quickly with a London accent and school English is a little different to conversational English.

It has only come home to me what an inhuman beast the German is since I have seen and had first hand information of the way he behaves to other nationalities. To him anybody other than a German is only fit to eat with pigs.

If the Germans had come into our house to loot I am sure Dad would be dead by now for he would never have stood by and seen his house turned upside down and soldiers taking everything they fancy.

I now have another book, the 'Second Century of Humour', all short stories by good authors, H. G. Wells, P. G. Wodehouse, Mark Twain, Ian Hay, Charles Dickens and W. M. Thackeray etc.

### Wednesday 8 November 1944

The days seem to pass very quickly and if Monty doesn't hurry up I'll not be home for Christmas. Three months away from home is quite long enough for me. John seems very bothered over Roosevelt's election, personally I don't care whether Dewey wins or not, but I think Roosevelt has the public favour.

I wonder if Dad thinks me dead, I hope not, for it is no easy thing to think that of ones eldest son.

If the bombing of London is still on the children should be in Manchester, I hope they are satisfied with their billets, and Mother still existing in Wales. My appetite is enormous.

### Thursday 9 November 1944

Life is very enjoyable in some ways, but I must continually be on the alert for any Jerries breaking in here. He always seems to pick under my window for parking trucks and gets me looking for my exit.

I am now boiling my pullover that needed a wash. In front of my window is the Velperplein, it is like an ornamental park or recreation ground about the size of Ducketts Common, zig-zagged across it are numerous trenches.

I was up early this morning, lit my stove for toast at breakfast time and started reading Somerset Maughan's 'The Vessel of Wrath'. I am smoking home-grown tobacco, for cigarettes were rationed here and are now unobtainable. It smokes very quickly.

### Friday 10 November 1944

The days seem to fly by, it is all sleeping and eating. It is a long night from 6pm until 8am, and I sleep fitfully. The only trouble is that after a few hours there is very little fresh air in the hole and unpleasant to sleep in. I have cut up a dozen or more tobacco leaves for my pipe.

I had a few alerts dinner time when I thought Jerry was trying to break in. I am beginning to feel fit but my face of course is very pale through this indoor life.

Churchill has at last spoken of the V2 about two months late. I hope all is well at home for I remember hearing of the damage one did in Walthamstow. The boys now have yellow armbands allowing them in Arnhem for another month.

### Saturday 11 November 1944

Armistice Day 1944, and I did not hold the two minutes silence, for it did not enter my head. Jerry kept a 15 minute silence outside, but at that time I was trying to get a British army wireless set working but all in vain.

I feel greatly indebted to these people that are sharing their food with me for only bread and butter rations are buyable in town.

I have an egg regularly for tea, sometimes fried, sometimes boiled according to my wish. It is very worrying for these people to remain in town for the German can turn the remaining civvies out at anytime. My first year without a poppy.

### Sunday 12 November 1944

I have had a very pleasant day for I now have a small radio

to listen to. John and Pop have managed to get the electricity through to this house. I have heard the news about six times already and keep hoping to hear Arnhem mentioned. I heard 'Radio Arnhem Calling' break in on the AEF programme and give the German's news just as the British news was to begin.

I had another bath in a stand up fashion this morning. Last night for tea and supper I ate 12 slices of bread, four apples and quite a few biscuits and was still hungry, so tonight I have boiled myself some potatoes. Our bombers visited the Reich last night and passed over here for ack ack was very intense.

## Monday 13 November 1944

Tonight there is a fire raging in town, a hosiery warehouse minus its goods was set alight by the Bosch this afternoon in the next street. The electricity was cut off this afternoon and I thought my luxuries of electric light and radio were gone but this evening it came on again.

I heard the midnight news last night and at 7am this morning but I shall know before the radio when the Arnhem front flares up. Tomorrow is Tuesday so perhaps there will be some good news.

Our mum remarked how my cheeks had filled out and that I eat as much as Martin and John together. I certainly feel fit on the food. I do hope all at home are well.

## Tuesday 14 November 1944

Yes, it is Tuesday my exciting day right enough, but the excitement started earlier than expected. My story starts at 7.40pm last evening. I had been reading and was just going to eat my supper and listen to 'Monday Night at Eight' when I heard someone in the house. I immediately put my light out and waited for the footsteps to come into my room and then came the 'V' tap on my trap door, it was John.

I had to accompany him immediately to the Bank, I had no time to dress so went in the rain in stockinged feet. The fire had spread and was only one building separating the fire from here.

The air was thick with falling smudges and the place was a livid orange and red glow. I knew nothing about it in the hole. We expected it to take No. 7 (my house) and spread to the bank two houses further on, so everybody prepared to evacuate. I helped pack bedding and food onto a hand cart and at 9.30pm took them out in the street and I walked with John on one side of the cart and a decent Jerry came to help on the other, we changed sides quickly.

I say the Jerry was decent for helping these people move their belongings, not because he knew I was an Englishman. We were having difficulty in pushing the cart uphill under the railway bridge to make the Apeldoorn road on an icy road. I certainly sweated in case he spoke to me. John kept up a conversation with him so I was quite safe.

The new house was at No. 16 Sonsbeek Weg, and while the boys went back for more articles I stayed with another Dutch family, a man and wife and two daughters, they seemed very pleased to entertain a Tommy until all was ready to move in next door. We conversed together in smatterings of German, French, English and Dutch and with an English/Dutch dictionary we did marvels. Of course they expected me to tell them the exact date the offensive would start, but I did not let on.

They found some English records for me and one was 'The Lambeth Walk' recorded by Billy Cotton, they had no need to tell me that gramophone needles were unobtainable. At 11pm John came and said the fireman had checked the fire and did not think it would spread to No. 7, so with that good news we pushed the cart back.

At the Bank there was a crowd of Jerries but I pulled my overcoat collar up, my hat down and went through the middle and straight inside the Bank. With Pop I went into the basement and we talked in the light of a flickering candle.

He is 58 and has twice been taken away by the Gestapo, once for four days for not disclosing the names of people he had sold wireless sets to, and again for six weeks for trying to help Elizabeth's mother escape.

He joined the Dutch Navy when 13, about 1900, and

travelled the world as a radio operator. His home town is Leiden, a coastal town.

They came to Arnhem ten years before the war and set up an electrical business. During the course of conversation we indulged in a glass of wine and a quiet smoke just like two old men, afterwards the wine was replenished. The girls worked ceaselessly until 2am clearing up again when we all retired. These girls would show some English girls up for working.

It is incredible the amount of faith these Dutch folk have in the Tommy freeing Arnhem eventually. The fire has put an end to my electricity. I returned to my hole at 9.30 the next morning.

### Wednesday 15 November 1944

The radio described the weather in Holland as filthy the other day and it is still the same. Roads are continually wet and visibility nil.

I have all my belongings packed ready to take in case I have to leave again in a hurry for on Monday I left everything except my revolver. I accidentally rose at 7.15 instead of 8.15 this morning but I did not miss the hour as I was asleep by 6.30 last night.

I have been cleaning and sharpening my sheath knife today. I have also cut up more tobacco leaves. Mark Twain is very humorous. *(That knife is now on show in the Airborne Museum at Oosterbeek).*

### Thursday 16 November 1944

The sun has shone today and it is quite a cold but pleasant day. Artillery has been very active but I still reckon on another fortnight at least before we are freed. Pop has been very clever with the German, for in September he was just a shopkeeper but now he has made himself 'Town Electrician' and has the confidence of the Germans. He has a gang of boys working for him, all the Underground boys of whom most know nothing of electricity, it is just a blind to keep them in the town and with the passports they now have, cannot be taken for trench digging elsewhere. This time last year I was a tank man at Barnard Castle. I wonder where I shall be this time next year, in civvie street I hope. I shall have hopes of getting home by Christmas just as Monty promised, until it is past.

## Friday 17 November 1944

Throughout the night and today an artillery duel has raged. The local Dutch news is good: a pontoon bridge at Oosterbeek broke when a tank was in the middle with the result that the tank is useless and traffic held up for some time. Heavy materials, tanks and guns etc., are being brought across the Rhine to this side.

A Tank Regiment passed through town last night after dark in the direction of Germany. Weather once again is cold and wet. The second offensive has started in Holland today but in Limburg again.

John went cadging for bread this morning and managed 10lb of bread, for there are three other people besides myself without ration books.

## Saturday 18 November 1944

The day has passed extremely quickly, for I now have two comrades who are going to live here. They belong to Pop's electricians and must all move within a small area. One called Klaas is sleeping here tonight, and Nico is coming tomorrow.

A would-be deserter from the German Army asked Martin to help him through to the British lines, there is a sure sign of rot in their ranks.

A fighter sweeping low over the town this afternoon shot three German officers dead, they were in a car. There are numerous parties of Jerries passing through the town with heavy packs and food store. They are going eastwards and northwards to Germany. Artillery still very heavy.

## Sunday 19 November 1944

For the first time in Holland I slept in a proper bed. It was so lovely and warm at 10pm that I completely stripped off and found a pair of pyjamas.

I had a very humorous evening with Klaas and the Dutch/English dictionary, he knows some English words but cannot put them into an intelligent sentence.

Martin has once again resumed the role of barber and is making good progress towards becoming a pro. It was a glorious clear day for aircraft but only a few came near here.

Since I have been here I have remembered that Mum, Dad, Gran and Grandad have had their birthdays. I have a genuine excuse this year to forget. I have had some Edgar Wallace and Ellery Queen's detective literature sent me by a young lady named Truus from Arnhem.

A diary like this definitely justifies a dedication, it of course goes to Joan of whom I am always thinking. I also write in the knowledge that my father a 1914-1918 ex-Middlesex Regiment soldier will be most interested.

### Monday 20 November 1944

Last night Klaas brought quite an important personage to sleep instead of Nico. He was a man of 50 who owns quite a few shops in Arnhem. He has lost through looters about £15,000 of goods including all his motor cars. He brought a bottle of wine and a box of cigars so now I have a cigar and wine for lunch. His wife cooked a woodcock (like a wood-pigeon) for me, and with boiled potatoes it went down very well. It was as tender and as tasty as chicken.

Afterwards a bowl of stewed apples and some short-cake fancies. I also had a clean set of underclothes today, so I feel as if in a manger and receiving gifts of incense.

A British soldier was found dead in one of the houses by the Rhine, the Underground buried him, a William Reeve. Reeve was a member of A Company of my Battalion and probably the soldier I saw laid out on a wall on the Sunday afternoon.

### Tuesday 21 November 1944

I am one of the very few people who has ever shaken hands with the diggers of his grave. The two policemen that found me in the police building told other policemen that I was

78

dead when they first went down. One told Nico and Klaas who went to the Rhine and dug a grave for the poor chap, they came back and spent two hours in the Police building from 2pm until 4pm searching for my body.

I had left at 1.30pm. We all thought it very funny. What a coincidence! They are no more electricians than I am, but have passports to stay in the town as such. They are both active Underground and are both wanted by the Gestapo for evading going to work in Germany for two years. Klaas was a cabinet maker and Nico a bread baker.

I had another humorous evening with the English lessons, both are keen to learn and it was 12.30am before we said Goodnight.

### Wednesday 22 November 1944

Tonight I have prepared an assortment of vegetables for a hot-pot for when the lads come. Nico has brought a quarter pound of tea bought by a friend through the Black Market at 200 guilders a pound (£20), some German sausage, pork fat (known as bacon here) also at a high price through the Black Market, cheese, butter, sugar and bread, so I once again have

The author, left, in civilian clothes at Velperplein Arnhem, with Resistance worker Nico van den Oever.

a larder, it is for our evening meal and I am the cook.

Jerry has taken all the paper money from the Bank today but the lads have hidden the gold. Nico awoke at 6am this morning and recited his English lessons, they are certainly keen. They all have ambitions of soldiering. I'll cure them!

### Thursday 23 November 1944

After nearly a month of gorging, I am right on top of my six week hunger strike! These Dutch boys of military age have better stories than me to tell of dodging Jerry, for Klaas lived in a compartment between two rooms with two other chaps. Nico in three different hiding places in two years, seeing their parents about once a week during daylight. Also John who never saw the streets for 15 months.

The Gestapo left Arnhem in September when the fighting started. A civvie told me that the town is now well fortified with trenches being dug all round the town. I hope it starts soon for I have had a good holiday from the army and am now ready to start soldiering again.

### Friday 24 November 1944

The weather has been dreadful lately and artillery spasmodic. We want some cold dry weather before the tanks will be any good in this country.

One story has it that we send patrols quite frequently during the dark hours to this side of the Rhine and one clashed with a German patrol. Nico was talking to a Jerry with a sten gun wound in his hand. Nico and Klaas have worked the oracle by getting two ration cards each, one for where they eat, and one for use here.

Last night we had egg and bacon, we would just call it fat, but it is all they ever see and then only through the Black Market at a high price. When the bacon was cooked, three eggs were scrambled over it, then when cooked, cut into three. They are all for things being mixed or mashed together.

### Saturday 25 November 1944

At 6.30am this morning I made the fire up for an early morning cup of tea, my comrades prepared themselves in stolen police uniforms to proceed to Apeldoorn to visit their parents and friends 20 miles away, for only policemen are allowed out of town. They fit the part well for are about five feet nine inches and keep the uniforms smart.

The prospects were cheering this afternoon for with shelling, bombing and aircraft shooting, the building shook at times. Nico proudly showed me a British gas-cape from the police building this morning and it has just dawned on me that it must be mine for I know exactly what equipment was left there. Someone has been at my kit. John and Martin are sleeping here tonight with me.

### Sunday 26 November 1944

Last night began a series of aircraft activities which carried on throughout the night and today. The day is quite sunny. John says quite a lot of Jerries were killed by aircraft on the Rhine yesterday.

One of our bombers was brought down by ack ack fire over Apeldoorn, six men baled out but Jerry shot them all while coming down.

I was politely told today that I have been eating horsemeat, I was horrified at first but it is only a little tougher than tough steak. Not many more days to Christmas. I wonder if I'll be in England by then. I am quite fat in the face now.

### Monday 27 November 1944

Today has been very exciting. To start with we had a young lady visitor last night who stayed the night and of which very little more will be said. This morning Klaas and Nico went to my old hideout for the remnants of my kit and while coming away, quite loaded, a Jerry stopped them and asked to see inside. (There was only a battledress inside one case). They sweated and explained it was police equipment and they got away with it.

Today Jerry came back to the Bank searching for the gold. In the safe was 100 Underground armbands, we all had fits, for if they were discovered, all the men would be shot without trial.

John's girl walked in, picked up the parcel and strolled over and gave them to me. Martin was a chalky white for the next hour. They have taken the caretaker away with them, for what reason we know not. My boots and jumping smock are missing from my uniform.

## Tuesday 28 November 1944

We now have electricity once again so have no need for the carbide lamp or the oil lamp, we also have the wireless. The weather is very bad, it rained all day.

While Nico was in Velp this afternoon a piece of shrapnel from a shell just missed him. The caretaker from the Bank has not returned today and his wife is very tearful. I fully understand her feelings.

It is four weeks since I left the police building and the police-belt the boys recovered for me now fits me whereas in the police building was far too loose. I had my photo taken with Klaas and Nico today for Nico is an amateur photographer.

## Wednesday 29 November 1944

We had excellent company last evening in the shape of Paul one of the boys from Under. He is the editor, producer and publisher of 'The Daily World News' a foolscap sheet stencilled on a typewriter and in its second year. It now has a publication of 300 copies each printing. He is very clever and speaks English very well, it was his sister Truus that sent me the books and a note. He explained the situation thoroughly.

During the whole time I have been in Arnhem British troops have never been more than three miles away and at the moment are by the blown railway bridge about one mile away, but only a patrol in small numbers.

We hold the south bank of the Rhine for about ten miles in the Westerly direction. We discussed the possibility of crossing the river and getting to the British lines.

It means over an hour in the river and the risk of mines and booby traps. Patrols across the river are frequent. During the first fortnight that I was in the police building 50 of our boys were helped across the river by the Underground and he reckons another 100 are in the villages around with civilians but I am the only one in Arnhem. The next of kin of most of them know they are safe!

Another Englishman was found in a burnt house. All his papers were burnt so I haven't his name! I heard, 'If You Like a Ukelele Lady' on the wireless today, memories, Mum and Dad!

### Thursday 30 November 1944

The news is excellent today. Advances everywhere along the front except the Second Army in Holland. The Rhine is fast flowing and flooding banks already, so it may overflow this year. I hope to bring a piece of black bread back with me just to compare with ours and at the moment is better than before since all the people are evacuated and there are only a few people to bake for. It is as solid as a rock and a loaf weighs 6 lb compared to our 2 lb.

I now have a small arsenal in my hole for our next battle, with sten guns, ammunition and grenades. Nico brought about 8 lbs of plastic explosive from the Underground today.

I have been showing my comrades how plastic explosives should be used but more importantly the need to keep their personal weapons clean. Jerry has now begun to fortify the interior of the town and three emplacements for MGs are in this square, so I will be in the thick of it.

Nico is in his element taking photographs of their positions, also the stealing of lorry loads of furniture. A Jerry officer wanted to take John's girl away with him to cook for him (as if she can cook!).

### Friday 1 December 1944

Martin came to visit me last night and we talked and listened to the wireless together. We have very much in common. Klaas was firefighting, for Jerry lit up three fires during the early evening. Nico slept at Onder der Linden for he could not leave the girl in the house by herself. (This is the girl we think gave away the whole LKP group to the Germans).

She had come from Apeldoorn and wanted to get to the British lines for Red Cross work. Nico said it was impossible so she begged to stay with him, he couldn't tell her he lived here with me so stayed at Klaas' house and is going to take her to Mr Speyer where he normally eats in the morning.

Workmen have started taking the tram shelter down opposite my house, it is either for another strong point or is an obstruction for them. Lorries and carts are ceaselessly taking goods from this town, only the bare walls of the town stand, and they'll be knocked down when the fighting starts.

### Saturday 2 December 1944

As soon as Nico arrived back last night he went firefighting for this time Jerry had set light to the Gas Works. Nico did not get in until past midnight. Klaas slept at Mr Speyer's for they have now moved him about 3 miles away, he was told to evacuate his house.

Lucy, a girl of 27 who I have been writing to has had to go to Velp with her young man. I heard Donald Peers sing, 'By a Babbling Brook', last night, it brought back memories of the Wood Green Empire. I have a letter for a person in England from my pen friend.

A Jerry stole Nico's bike yesterday while he was moving Mr Speyer, so he cannot go to Apeldoorn and see his parents today. We are all very dissatisfied with waiting for nearly three months for the return of the Tommy, and hope he comes soon.

### Sunday 3 December 1944

There is a big check up in the Arnhem area today, soldiers are cordoning off residential suburbs, searching for unauthorised people and those who could be sent off to work in Germany. Nico and Klaas just missed the roundup.

For supper last night we three ate a piece of fried steak and some custard I made. This evening Klaas has cycled to Apeldoorn for he has many letters to post for the people of Arnhem and to give the 'Daily World News' to the population.

There is a law that all policemen under 40 must be 25 miles behind the front line, in case they go against Jerry. A large gun is stationed on the green outside since last night, it has been shaking this house. Aircraft were over this morning and ack ack was heavy.

My nerves are getting back to the police building state, listening for Jerry to break in. I do hope the lads come soon for a senior Jerry officer is trying to get all the civilians away from this area. The caretaker returned unheralded last night, his wife nearly had hysteria.

I have just finished copying the original writing of the first ten weeks into this new book, for the old book was in pencil and completely filled.

After three weeks I called that book 'Fugitive from a Prisoner of War Camp', but now with my later stages that title doesn't suffice for I am now in civilian clothes and will be shot as a spy if captured.

My original introduction ran: 'I have been in hiding for exactly three weeks today. I have no idea whether the British Forces will manage to push as far as Arnhem in three days, when my water runs out and then I must take to the roads and hope for the best. I have not had anything substantial to eat since breakfast on Sunday 17th September which I am sorry to say I brought up in the plane coming over'.

## Monday 4 December 1944

Last night Klaas went to Apeldoorn despite everybody's efforts to stop him, for on Saturday 5,000 men were carted off to Germany from there. He dressed up as a policeman and went in pouring rain, he has bags of guts. He had with him the Underground newspaper and passports for a dozen chaps to show exemption from German military work.

This house must be one of the very few that hasn't been broken into during the past five weeks, on the window is a notice from the Commander of the town saying nothing is to be stolen from here. They can't be trusted! Nico had not arrived by 11pm last night. I waited for the shootout, so I just took my shoes off and lay on the bed with my revolver handy for I didn't fancy undressing and being unready alone in the house. Troops were moving about outside.

Martin is cheerful, he reckons we will be free by February.

Martin Penseel
*Going to be friends for life!*

Police Lt. Hans van Maris
*My first Underground contact.*

Nico van den Oever
*We were friends for life!*

Klass Schuttinga
*A sensitive character.*

## Tuesday 5 December 1944

The weather brightened up today and several aircraft passed over. Nico is out tonight cementing up a basement of furniture to prevent Jerry stealing it, if they have to move quickly. It is bad news about our positions being flooded between Nijmegen and Arnhem, but the rest of the front is good.

The Maas at Venlo is 170 yards wide in flood so perhaps they will have to wait for spring to get across. The two boys are going to Amsterdam tomorrow for two days, cycling 60 miles each way for the Underground. Helping people evade the Germans seems to be their main concern in life. The radio has announced that our troops are being given seven days leave to the UK at the New Year, at that rate there will not be any offensive until they all return, about March.

## Wednesday 6 December 1944

Klaas went to Otterlo yesterday about six miles to the North to bring two of the boys from there into Arnhem with false passports, he had not returned by 11.30pm so I went to bed.

Nico had been in bed since 9.30 for they were supposed to be going to Amsterdam at 6am this morning. He was not here by morning so the Amsterdam journey was cancelled, everybody was worried in case Jerry had picked him up with his pistol on him. This evening he turned up full of smiles (just like I shall when I return home)! He stayed a few moments and had to return there, with some other papers to hinder the German war machine.

He brought news that a fortnight ago 130 Englishmen were helped across the Rhine by the movement but last week 137 were caught in a body trying to do the same. As I write the ack ack has opened up on our bombers going to bomb Germany no doubt.

## Thursday 7 December 1944

Osnabruck was our target last night and every aircraft that went passed over this house by the sound they made.

Martin slept in here last night as Nico was taken bad at Mr

Speyer's and Klaas was still away. I had a scare last night at 7.40, when all alone I heard somebody banging on the back door downstairs. I waited for the break-in, but they did not enter. I shall be absolutely white haired before I reach home.

I was hoping to be home by Christmas but now I think I'll be lucky to get home for my 21st. I can hold out here with this family so long as they have permission to stay at the Velperplein. I have a wonderful existence here for at seven each morning I see to the fire and then clear up, prepare breakfast, read, smoke and observe Jerry movements on the Velperplein, from my loft. (One would not think I was a penniless private).

### Friday 8 December 1944

Nico arose from his sick-bed today and must see a doctor about some liver trouble. The two boys fetched my stock of half a dozen hand grenades from the police building this afternoon that our chaps had left there. Several aircraft have flown over the town very low today, and the weather has been brighter.

I had two heavy attacks of nose bleeding during the night. Good living? Martin reckons it is smoking doing it, so I haven't smoked so far today and feel as if I want a pipe just now. According to hear-say, the water level is going down a little on the Rhine.

It is a very poor show on the part of those Greeks to battle with us, their liberators. Our second Parachute Brigade from Italy went to Athens and were caught up in a political battle with the Communists.

### Saturday 9 December 1944

We drank two litre bottles of wine last night between four of us, Martin, Klaas, Nico and myself. Nico was a little intoxicated but there wasn't much alcohol in it so I just slept well. I don't care for the taste of this wine at all.

This morning there was a heavy frost on the ground so another month of good dry weather may see an offensive in this direction. I now have a German passport to allow me to stay in Arnhem but hope I never have need to use it.

The radio is very cheering and takes my memory back to some pleasant dances with Joan. The boys have gone off to Apeldoorn this afternoon to see their parents and to deliver the newspaper etc.

Every evening at 7pm I listen to Radio Arnhem on 377 metres, it comes from the building opposite here, 50 yards away. They call the programme 'Jerry Calling', the serious news talks make me laugh, they only have old records and about 6 people run the programme.

### Sunday 10 December 1944

I now have another worry for after a husband has been posted as missing for so many months (three or six I think) the wife's family allotment ceases and she draws a considerably reduced amount in the shape of a widows pension. Anyway I hope that doesn't happen.

I shall have many more difficulties to overcome before I eventually reach home, especially about next March (let's hope before) when the Spring offensive goes in. For when this part of the town is being fought for and mortar bombs are whizzing about it will be uncomfortable here. We could be quite busy.

If anybody had told me after three weeks that I'd still be here after three months I should never had believed them. Martin once again has given me the shorn sheep appearance. The weather is brighter again and artillery livened up this afternoon.

### Monday 11 December 1944

The days seem to pass very quickly now that it is dark at 5pm of an evening. The dam about six miles away has been bombed and water is flooding through a 100 yard gap over German positions there.

Nico and Klaas have returned from their weekend trip today and have brought two rabbits back for me to cook for our supper. Martin now comes in each evening, just in case the other two don't arrive and sleeps with me in a single bed, it is a tight squeeze.

I am longing for the day when I reach home and all this

suspense will be over. I hope the offensive goes in before Spring for otherwise all at home will have written me off.

### Tuesday 12 December 1944

Times are very bad for food in Holland, for instance babies at Apeldoorn receive 1 oz of sugar a week and the other people nil. Butter or fat is now down to half-an-ounce a fortnight for there are no trains or transport of any description.

A letter took three weeks to come 60 miles. I have been lucky to get with people that have taken plenty of food in. They have not seen tea or chocolate since 1940 and as for bread, well I've mentioned that before.

Nico called into the Police station today, he brought back with him some more ammunition I had collected in my corner and a jump smock that one other had taken off. It still had a smell of cordite about it. It reminded me of the noise and shouting that went on that afternoon.

One of our aircraft bombed an evacuation hotel full of Arnhem people, 32 have been found dead out of 52.

### Wednesday 13 December 1944

Once again we had a shake on today for in one area of Arnhem there was a round up of everybody from the houses and herded into a church. They have stayed there all day long being interviewed one by one and if not in possession of an Ausweis (voucher of identity) for Arnhem, went out of the town today. Klaas and Nico were caught in that area.

I forgot to put on record that two German aircraft flew over Arnhem for the first time since I have been here, everybody thinks it a geographical mistake.

It is a coincidence that they should play on the radio today 'Spring will be Late this Year', just when I hope for an early spring offensive. The boys did not care a lot for my stewed rabbit, they always have it fried.

### Thursday 14 December 1944

The round up yesterday was more important than I first thought, for after carefully combing the houses they found a

Dutch SS soldier hiding and within two hours they had shot him. What a law in these parts, in England it would take six months to get an order to shoot a deserter, if they could. Today, Herman (the brother of Paul and Truus) came to develop Nico's films, including some that I found in the police building and for curiosity sake am having them developed.

There are some photos of me that Nico took and they look as if they will print well tomorrow morning when Herman will commence work on them. I find W. Somerset Maughan quite an interesting author.

## Friday 15 December 1944

This morning some of the films were printed and they came out quite well, me in particular, of course. During the day at intervals artillery has been quite heavy.

There is a local rumour going around that Jerry may evacuate Holland and fall back into a defensive line in Germany. I hope so, for I don't relish another two or three months creeping about listening for suspicious noises. It is better than being in a POW camp or in another world by far. I am a very pale colour due to three months inside a building.

When I went to shut my outside shutters for the blackout this evening I felt the wintry wind for the first time this year. Four Tommies stayed at a house in Arnhem in September and afterwards were passed on by the Underground.

They left their weapons in the house but Klaas and Nico could not find them there this afternoon. There were three more Jerry made fires in Arnhem last night, Klaas and Herman went out to fight them.

## Saturday 16 December 1944

The war has at last come to Arnhem again, but not in the form I had hoped. At about 20 minute intervals throughout the day V1s have buzzed over very very low, in fact lower and louder than those I heard in London, but strange to say I am not bothered. I believe they are being fired from the northern outskirts of Arnhem and are not travelling very far behind our lines.

Nico has gone to Apeldoorn again today to visit his parents but Klaas is not feeling too good, has spent the day in bed. Yesterday Nico was on his way to Velp on a borrowed cycle (for he had two of his own, and a friend's, stolen by the Germans in a fortnight). When a soldier stopped him and demanded his cycle, Nico showed him his Ausweis saying that he was of the Technica and nobody should have his cycle.

The soldier said it mattered nothing and took his cycle. On the way back he stole one from a German, who opened fire on his fleeing body, anyway he had another cycle. The height of humiliation describes Nico's feelings.

On Wednesday Lucy (my pen friend) was put in a cell in the police station at Velp for not having the German Ausweis to live there. At that time she had in her possession a letter from me which she ate and another to me which she burnt after finding some matches. She was kept there for four hours.

The weather is awful, it is pouring a heavy rain that can only be equalled by a Pacific monsoon. I am certainly missing some terrible weather through being indoors through October, November and December.

This is the second night without electricity. I miss the news and especially the 'Jerry Calling' programme from Bremen every evening at 7pm. During the day the family have moved from the Bank at No. 9 to another Bank next door No. 6.

The three old ladies from the Bank have moved in down-stairs and will provide me with food from now onwards. They lost their house in the fire of Arnhem in September. One is 79 and still going strong. Some Germans have been here tonight enquiring who lives here and whether they are Technicas and have the Ausweis etc. Aren't I lucky to have one?

### Sunday 17 December 1944

It is three months today since I last saw England and nearly the same since I spoke to an Englishman. I know and speak a little Dutch which seems to amuse everybody especially my pronunciation. Three women, the mother and two daughters provided an excellent dinner for me today, fried meat, brussels sprouts and enough boiled potatoes to have some to fry for tea. I am now so heavy that I am starting to take exercises with Klaas each morning, this life suits me, no responsibility for the military situation. A V1 fell in Arnhem last night about two miles away.

### Monday 18 December 1944

It gives me a great sense of satisfaction to close the wooden shutters outside my windows each evening and watch a Jerry labour Battalion marching back to their quarters singing lustily of their Fatherland. They would be after my blood if they knew my nationality. Klaas has gone off to see his parents at Apeldoorn and Nico has not arrived back from his weekend trip yet. I wonder how the folks at home will spend Christmas, thinking of me no doubt. If Tommy comes tomorrow I might get home for Christmas.

### Tuesday 19 December 1944

The days seem to pass quickly but it seems ages since I was in the police building and yet only seven weeks ago today.

The German counter offensive in the Ardennes, is quite serious reaching 20 miles into Belgium already, just at this crucial news' moment the electricity fails again. The V1 comes over very low quite regularly night and day. All the German parachutists in the town left today for another front, there is nothing doing here for them.

I have decided that I am due for 14 days' leave once I return to England. My pals have been POWs for three months today!

### Wednesday 20 December 1944

Nico brought news last night from a friend of his of revolts and strikes in all the big towns under German rule in Holland owing to the food shortage. They have one and a half pounds (600 gr) of bread and two pounds of potatoes weekly, no butter or sugar etc. This friend had cycled from The Hague.

About a dozen V1s have already dropped short of the front lines a few miles north of Arnhem. They seem to go between the chimney pots. The news is blacked out from Belgium but am very interested in how serious it gets before being checked.

**Thursday 21 December 1944**

The boys brought in two excellent wireless sets from a house Jerry had left. All the troops seem to be moving down to the real battlefront.

There have been several big explosions lately and this house has rocked on its foundations. Today I ate goat meat, for Jerry gave father a whole goat when the battalion left.

**Friday 22 December 1944**

I now have an authentic Dutch and German passport, the name is Kaastens, Jacobus Hendrick.

According to America this latest offensive will shorten the war, but how Jerry will win the war for us by taking the offensive is just a little confusing to me. Thirty five miles into Belgium is a long way to push them back.

Several more explosions have shaken this building today. I now know all the latest songs as I have the wireless going nearly all day, 'Put the Cat out Tonight', is the catchiest tune. Minny is now going to write to Joan through the Red Cross.

**Saturday 23 December 1944**

Once again the sun made an effort to show itself today, and now the roads are quite dry and the clouds a light blue. The radio reports intense patrol activity across the Maas in Holland. I am disgusted with a spelling bee where parents against their children could not spell phlox and a mother had never heard of philatelist.

A member of the Underground who was free for four days at Osterbeck with our Division HQ came yesterday, he was responsible for getting the men back across the Rhine, he said the Diviion is now in England, at least the 2,000 that are left. He knew what he was talking about, I think he came to check on me.

94

They may have been occupied but they were never conquered.

One blind lady does her best to show her resistance to the common enemy.
Three silk bookmarks given to me on my 21st birthday.

## Sunday 24 December 1944

Christmas Eve 1944, and hard, though I have tried by putting holly around the room and joining in the carol singing over the radio, I cannot get the spirit of Christmas. The old lady downstairs with her two daughters (43 and 47) are very good in giving me cups of tea, and coffee every morning. At this time my thoughts are more than ever centred at home (number one word in my vocabulary) and how all must be worried.

To kiss Joan and have a handshake from Dad are the two moments I look forward to for I expect Mum will still be away in Wales and I shall not see her for some time. I am very pleased with the weather, the sun shone beautifully all day.

## Monday 25 December 1944

Christmas Day, this morning I gave the three boys their tea and biscuit in bed at 7am, then we all slept until 10am when we started decorating in earnest. The boys had brought a Christmas tree in from Apeldoorn and Martin took the branches from one side and we nailed it on the wall, it was four feet high

With the other sprigs he made small branches around the room mingled with the holly. The tree looked very good, with tinsel, varied coloured glass balls and red candles.

During the morning I received an invitation frm Marin to dine out at the Bank, on the opposite corner. It is the first time I have ever accepted a written invitation and straight away put an automatic in my pocket for the occasion, for I believe in safety first. As soon as I arrived I had morning coffee at 1pm.

Martin, father and I retired to an underground room, very small but very comfortable, furnished with a small round table and four armchairs, along one wall was a radiogram which entertained us with English records, while we had some German wine Krausenbitter, guaranteed to rot anybody's stomach, it was very strong.

Needless to say I did not reject the offer of two replenishments. Then came dinner, vermicelli soup, green peas, young carrots, meat and ample potatoes. For dessert, lemon blancmange, it ended in true Dutch protestant style by Mevrou (Mrs) reading a passage from the Bible. Elizabeth, the Jewish girl of seven years, that the family are looking after, took a fancy to me, so for the rest of the day she stuck to me like a good-un.

She, like most young Jewess's has a very attractive face, big blue eyes and jet black hair, her parents were taken away to Poland three years ago and killed it is believed, for nothing more has been heard of them.

With the radiogram playing dance music I danced with Baby, she is 28 and engaged to John.When all were settled the Christmas presents were given out, all things that had been found in Arnhem by the boys for there are no shops to buy anything.

I made a large parcel up of an armband that came from the Police building, after ten wrappings it took Elizabeth ten minutes to untie. I also had four presents much to my surprise, one was a coat hook on a Boy Scout plaque, an eagle and a Royal Crest of Holland, forbidden to be displayed since 1940 by the Germans.

Tea was at 7.15, everybody had a plate of bread and butter, two with fried meat on, two of cheese and two sugared, it must be the habit as they have been used to so many slices per day to make the bread last the week.

About 9pm some coffee was served, then father, Martin and I resumed with the same wine, John on Hollands Gin and the five women on egg flip concoction, raw eggs and gin bottled. It is a good job that they did not understand my remarks on the effects.

Martin and I accompanied the records with impersonations of drums, cymbals and the strumming of the Big Brass (solo by Martin) and then my clarinet (cigarette paper and comb) broke forth. By this time I was livened up considerably and rendered Tipperary with many additions of my own.

The evening came to a close at 23.45 hours. I boldly walked back to our house with Martin, my automatic was put away and I realised what a few happy hours I had had, forgetting all my worries for a few hours.

I sincerely hope all at home forgot me for a little while and stopped worrying, enjoying themselves on this occasion.

### Tuesday 26 December 1944

Boxing Day has been one of good music and shows on the radio, with excerpts from the Palladium, 'Happy and Glorious' with Tommy Trinder, also Nervo & Knox at His Majesty's, I hope to see them all very shortly.

The two boys managed three and a half pound of beef (boneless) for 22 Guilder (50/-) through the Black Market. Also a Christmas present of two pounds of bacon that I boiled, it is very rare in Holland nowadays. They have some good acquaintances.

Martin had tea over here of bread and meat and we all had a blancmange I had made for supper. Mr Churchill is in Athens and nearly sat on three quarter ton of explosive. Very heavy frost this morning.

### Wednesday 27 December 1944

It is bitterly cold every morning with everywhere covered with a thick layer of frost just like snow. It is a good job I am out of that Police building or else I should be a stiff by now.

The artillery has improved in volume these last few days and Velp about 2 miles away has been shelled with each shell a yard farther on than the last. The boys went to Amsterdam this morning and aren't expected back until Friday evening.

### Thursday 28 December 1944

My heart missed a beat last night for a V1 seemed to stop directly over this house and very low, but there was no explosion, a dud I imagine. They are very frequent around here and take a S.W. direction which is roughly Antwerp from here about 100 miles.

Churchill has had a hectic time in Athens with dynamite, shelling and now snipers. For the first time for a week there was no frost this morning. I hope to read the papers dated September 18th to see what the public were told of usl

### Friday 29 December 1944

The roads have now turned to ice and a very heavy frost this morning did not help. Several aircraft have flown over and the ack ack opened up on them. If Jerry's idea of the break through was to reach Antwerp he was much nearer to cross the Maas in Western Holland, than he is now. For it is only 35 miles away and at the moment from the extreme tip of his offensive he has approximately 70 miles to go.

I hope to see the Canadians on this sector before the end of January but inside I know it is just wishful thinking for Spring is the time for an offensive. I reckon I could turn 11 stone on the scales easily now. I do miss good English soap.

BAD NEWS: At last we have had instructions to move to another part of the town. I dread it.

## Saturday 30 December 1944

The weather has turned bad once again after a week's lapse of good weather. Visibility is down to 100 yards, and I haven't yet shaken off my forlornness at having to move. If the boys can make a good hideout under the floorboards for me at the other house then I shall go there, otherwise at Otterloo (ten miles away) there is a place in some woods where some of the boys that went Under hid for two years. But here I am very comfortable, a stove, radio, books and electricity.

As I said three months ago, how much longer, or as the latest song would say, 'It Had To Be You'. At last we have pushed the tip of the salient back nine miles and in the Southern flank North of Bastogne narrowed it to 12 miles.

## Sunday 31 December 1944

We had planned that I should see the New Year in over in the Bank but as my Ausweis is for 1944 I must leave town tonight about 6pm when it is half dark to go to this hut in the woods. It is certainly very dangerous leaving town so I don't know where I shall be in seven hours time.

Martin burst into tears last night when telling me, he said he'd rather lose his mother or father than me, very touching. This morning mother came up and also had a little sob, so goodness knows how all at home are, I haven't known such tearful days since I told Joan I was going into the Army. The control over this town is now much tighter so I hope the boys can get me out without being challenged.

I hope I am in a position to write tomorrow's piece in this book and not with the Bosch. Everybody is very kind to me. I am all packed and am having dinner and tea over at the Bank - the Germans are over at the Bank so I have had dinner alone.

# CHAPTER FOUR

# 1 January 1945

*Cycle out of Arnhem and pass muster at the control post. Meet three Airborne men in a field, find an excellent host family.*

I FEEL greatly relieved for we made it last night. About eight o'clock Nico and Klaas turned up on their cycles at the bank and after saying goodbye to Mr & Mrs Penseel, John and Martin and our evacuee Elizabeth. I sat on the back carrier of Nico's cycle and we set off. I was only wearing a sports jacket with the collar turned up and it was a freezing cold night. There was a light layer of snow on the ground that had frozen and we crunched our way along, it was hard going for Nico, and on small inclines I had to get off and walk.

We each had a weapon in our pocket and a letter signed by the German Commandant of the town to say that we were important technicians in Arnhem. Mine was stamped 'deaf and dumb' and that was to be my act, until we were suspected.

We travelled about a mile before we were stopped at a road block. The German soldier yelled something like "Halt minche" (which means "Halt you so and so and show me your passport "), we pulled up and handed over our passes. The soldier just gave me a quick look and I put on the most sorrowful and inane expression I could muster.

Klaas and Nico gabbled away in German to the guard and after wishing him a happy New Year the barrier was lifted and we passed through.

I had a good look at the soldier and he appeared to be only a youth of 18-19 years and was frozen with the cold. His hat had been pulled over his ears and his greatcoat nearly reached the ground. Fortunately he was too cold and miserable to want to search us or to ask where we were making for. It was just a lucky break for us. We continued the journey without a word to each other as voices carried in the still night and English was not a popular language to be heard in occupied Holland.

Our objective was a road-house at Woeste-Hoeve about eight miles along the Apeldoorn road. On both sides of the road were small woods that cast eerie shadows in the moonlight.

On our left was the aerodrome Deelen that was supposed to have been captured intact for the RAF fighters the previous September. On the opposite side of the road a British fighter plane had crashed and was neatly suspended between two trees.

So far we had been lucky, and then in front of us we saw a soldier dragging a hand cart, it looked like stores for the aerodrome. When we got up to him he asked Nico to stop and wanted his cycle. Nico swerved away from him and shouted out that he could have it when Nico came back. We put on speed as it was downhill and got out of trouble.

Klaas had my attache case strapped on the back of his cycle. My diary, shaving kit and few souvenirs from Arnhem were in it.

We reached the road-house and I waited in the shadows while Nico and Klaas went to the back door and found Jan Himmerling.

Jan came out and said that the family had company and he did not want them to know of the Englishman, so we waited outside in the cold. Klaas and Nico had to be off back to Arnhem so we said goodbye and they wished me luck. I thanked them for all their help and said I hoped to meet them in England in the summer.

Jan and I stood talking for quite a while about the situation, the main topic being when would the liberation come, I stuck to my story of the Spring offensive.

Several German transports passed along the main road, but they kept going as I hoped they would.

About half a mile away in the woods a Russian soldier who had escaped from the Germans was hiding in a hut. It was a relief to me to hear that I was not going to be billeted with him for he did not speak a word of English. In one large room of this road-house were twenty Jews, all trying to keep alive until the liberation. If only Monty knew of the plight of these people he would hasten to their rescue.

At last the visitors left and I was able to go inside and warm up. A large meal was prepared and we all had a midnight feast. I had lived to see the New Year in. Could I live to see it out?

I slept with Jan and after breakfast we left for another rendezvous. He cycled about fifty yards in front of me and if he was stopped I was to double around and make for the road-house.

After half an hour of gentle riding we came to Hoenderlo, a small village well off the beaten track, and there I passed into the house of an ex-officer of the Dutch Army. He was away making arrangements for me to sleep the night elsewhere. Jan went back to the road-house.

During the morning a German fighter plane passed just over the housetops, the Luftwaffe had been on a low level attack on our communications in France and Belgium, it was a New Year effort. This was the last time I saw their aircraft.

In this semi-detached modern house that I had been brought to by Jan, I was introduced to Gerard, a young Dutchman who had been educated in England. This was marvellous as it was the first time for three and a half months that I could talk as fast as I liked and be understood without using sign language.

Gerard's sister also spoke English, so did the ex-officer's wife. During the day we had a few visitors, but no Germans, this seemed a lovely life and I was quite satisfied with myself.

The day passed quickly and after a good meal at 6.30 we waited for my next underground 'host'. He arrived at about eight o'clock in the evening and I left on foot with him to go to the next village of Otterlo.

I do not know the names of these people at Otterlo but

A U S W E I S .für Oktober 1944.
- - - - - - - -

Herr Bernardus Speijer
Paul Krugerstraat 26
A R N H E I M .
ist eingesetzt worden bei der
T E C H N I S C H E   N OT H I IF E
- - - - - - - - - - - - - -

für Strassenreinigung, Wiederherstel-
von Beschädigungen, Wasserlei-
tungsreparaturen u.s.w.  Gegebenen-
falls ist er tätig bei der Feuerwehr.
Arnheim, 12 Oktober 1944

Leutnant :
Aussenstelle Arnheim der
Wehrmachtkommandatur
Leutnant:

AUSWEIS for October 1944
Mr. Bernardus Speijer
Paul Krugerstraat 26
ARNHEIM
has been employed with the
TECHNICAL   EMERGENCY SERVICES
for street cleaning, making good
damage, water service  repair etc.
Given to him in case he is employed
by the Fire Brigade.

This was typed on thin veneer, there was a shortage of paper.
My ausweis carried a 'photo of me

104

once again they gave me a terrific welcome. The family consisted of three sons and a daughter between the ages of 20-30 and the mother and father. A supper had been prepared and once again I found an appetite.At five minutes to nine I was rushed upstairs into the bedroom and asked if I wanted to hear the nine o'clock news.

A part of the wall was pulled away to reveal a radio concealed behind a false partition. The Dutch folk do not lack ingenuity. The eldest son had overcome the lack of electricity by fixing up 2v battery bulbs all over the house and running them from an accumulator.

We only had one alert when the German patrol came round to check up on any lights showing outside the houses. We smoked and drank coffee until late and then retired. I had had a most interesting day.

After breakfast we went by cycle to a farmhouse where the parents had twenty-two children. I was just in time for 'elevenses' and by this time I had lost my desire for tea and had acquired the Dutch 'fresh ground coffee with milk' taste. At lunch I dined with the 'elders' in the parlour, the children used the kitchen.What a family to feed! They could only be fed on a farm.

On the way here we passed the remains of a German ammunition convoy, after our fighters had dealt with it. Huge shells of 88mm calibre, about 2ft 6in long stood all

My three Airborne companions with that very brave farmer, Herman van Esveld, John Haller, Harold Riley and Frank McNaught.

around and the remains of the lorries were spread over the neighbouring wood. At another spot I saw a V1 that had come down, unexploded, and was caught between the branches of three trees.

After meals the large and heavy family Bible was placed on the table in front of Ffather and he read a chapter, starting from where he left off the day before.

Before I left the gin was put on the table, and I was expected to drink with the elders. I shall never like the taste of gin. One of the sons took me on to another farmhouse where two 'higher ups' in the underground movement screened me.

Separately they questioned me on my English way of life, family, and where I had been in Holland. I convinced them that I was a genuine Englishman, but I did not tell them the names of the people in Arnhem that had helped me. They promised to let my wife know that I was safe, and said that they were in radio communication with England.

This news was a great relief to me for I was a little worried about how my family would take the news of my being missing. At last I was pronounced 'OK' and another chap came and took me in the dark across fields and footpaths to another farmhouse. He told me that I was to meet other Englishmen. I could hardly wait.We had to move carefully as there were many soldiers in the area and civilians were not supposed to be out after dark.

We arrived at the farmhouse at Kootwjkerbroek and were ushered in to the kitchen. There were no Englishmen present, they were on their way, but we managed some sort of conversation.

These people had been hiding Englishmen for some weeks and had picked up quite a few English phrases. There was a knock on the door and in came five queer looking men that surely could not be Englishmen.

They all wore wooden clogs and odd items of clothing and were of such varying heights (6 ft. odd to 5 ft and a few inches) that they looked like something out of a circus. They all greeted me in Dutch and I was bewildered. I was asked to pick out the Englishmen but I gave it up.

One by one they were introduced. John Haller was the tall Glider Pilot, Harold Riley was the very short Brigade signaller, a parachutist, Frank McNaught was a 4th Brigade parachutist, and Paul was a Dutch Secret Service Agent who had parachuted into Holland a month before we arrived, in September. The fifth man was their escort, a Dutch underground soldier.

We ate a hearty meal and then eagerly told each other our stories. It was soon past bedtime and I was told that they had a super hiding place. The snow lay thick on the ground and I was led out across the fields. We stopped in the middle of the field by the side of an innocent looking haystack. A large piece of wood had been placed against the side, this was removed and the farmer started pulling hay from the bottom of the stack. This revealed a hole leading into the hollow haystack, we crawled in, had a torch for a light. There was sufficient room inside for five to sleep in comfort.

The farmer closed the gap with hay and said he would see us in the morning with breakfast. This position reminded me of my childhood days when we would grope our way

The opening in the hollow haystack exposed. Five of us slept comfortably. At one end were shelves stacked with equipment that had been dropped to the Resistance. I took a pair of army trousers in my size and dyed them black.

The haystack is shown some years later when in a state of
disrepair. The wooden frame was camouflage for the entrance.

under rhododendron bushes and find small hide-outs in
the undergrowth.

At one end of our sleeping room was a rack stacked with
British battledresses, they had been dropped by the RAF for
chaps like myself. My size was there so I had new trousers.

We talked and talked last night until three o'clock this
morning, then we heard something moving outside the
haystack, we listened and stood ready to make a dash for it
in case the Germans set fire to the haystack.

It must have been a false alarm for I awakened to see the
farmer offering me some breakfast. Coffee with black bread
and egg sandwiches.

We laid on the straw covered ground talking and eventually
crawled out to have a good wash down and lunch in the
farmhouse. The farmer Herman van Esveld and his wife
were most charming people and did all they could to make
us comfortable.

It came as a blow to me to be told that we were over-
crowded and that I was to move that afternoon. I said
goodbye a little sorrowfully and walked across the fields with
another Dutchman to Essen, the neighbouring village.

The other Englishmen had warned me not to let the

Dutchmen know that I carried arms, as they would have confiscated them for their own use. Having had my automatic with me through so many escapades I was very much attached to it. I gave them my .38 revolver!

After a short, brisk walk we arrived at a large farmhouse, and there I was shown into a beautifully decorated parlour. I sat in a comfortable chair smoking my pipe and taking notice of all that went on around me. There seemed to me to be about fifty people staying there. They had been turned out of their homes at Arnhem and had been evacuated to this farm.

There was a family from Renkum (our dropping zone) who had had their farmhouse completely demolished and were seeking refuge for the time being. Several of the men had been taught English about 20 years previously at school, and they aired their 'knowledge' on me! I was told that someone would call for me during the evening to take me on my journey. To my delight I found that I was going to rejoin the Englishmen I had left in the haystack at Kootwijkerbrook.

A party had been arranged that evening at van Esveld's house and two Glider Pilots had been invited from another farm. That made six Englishmen. We were all very anxious to make a dash across the Rhine and get back to our troops. The last attempt was made in November. John and Harold had been on it but they were discovered by a German patrol and had had to make their own way back to this farmhouse, quite a few of the chaps had been taken prisoner.

The party was very jolly, there was plenty to eat and drink, and Herman van Esveld showed us his medals for running, and the rest of the family heirlooms. There were about twenty of us present. Before I left I handed my diary to van Esveld for safe keeping as it had too much information of value to the Germans if they captured it.

The rest of the story is now written from memory and a little note-book that I kept. It was quite late when we crept into the haystack to sleep.

After breakfast in the haystack I was told to get ready to leave for a permanent hide-out, until the journey over the

Rhine could be arranged. I was very sorry to leave the other Englishmen but as I was the last arrival I had to go to the new place.

I said goodbye to everybody and thanked van Esveld for his kindness.

A Dutchman came for me about midday and I followed him on a cycle for miles. We passed through the busy market town of Barneveld. An arrogant German soldier stepped straight off the kerb in front of my cycle, I braked sharply and rode round him, putting on speed in case he wanted my cycle.

We stopped in a farmyard where I was handed over to another Dutchman named Gerrit van den Munkhof, who was to take me on to my next farmhouse. This turned out to be Johan van Dijk's farm at Achterveld.

The van Dijk farmhouse at Achterveld was about half a mile from the centre of the village and Gerrit, the last underground man to escort me, showed me into the best room. It was a strange situation, just sitting and having coffee and home made biscuits, without being able to hold an intelligent conversation.

Neither van Dijk nor Gerrit could speak English and my Dutch was only "thanks", "no thanks", "after you", I am hungry and thirsty ", and a few other phrases

The van Dijk family, left to right: Mina, Johan, the author, a visitor and Jans the mother of the children.

which I had learnt. An English/Dutch dictionary was found and I managed to tell them my story helped by hand and arm gestures.

Van Dijk was a typical Dutchman, lanky and with a red shiny face, an extremely good temperament and aged about 35 years. He was in the Dutch Army in 1940 when the Germans over-ran the country, and after rounding them up the Germans took all their weapons and sent them home. (What a war, five days and them demobilised). During his eight years of marriage he had nine children including one set of twins.

The children were more than Mrs van Dijk could manage, and so Mina (van Dijk's sister) was employed to do the washing, cooking, bath the children and anything that occurred between 6 am and 10.30 pm.

There were also three other evaders on the farm but they were Dutchmen hiding from the Germans. All three were given their food and lodging on the farm in return for feeding cattle and sawing wood etc.

The eldest was Jacob, a man of 40 years, he was an Austrian Jew but had left his own country just before the purge, and was now a naturalised Dutchman. He had left his wife and son in s'Hertogenbosch which was in the British occupied area of South Holland. He could speak a little English.

Arie was abut 32, his wife lived in Amersfoort and came to visit him once a week. Arie did not like the idea of being found on the farm with an Englishman and told Johan van Dijk that I should leave. Johan made arrangements for Arie to become an onderdijker with another farm. What a strong character this Dutchman had, he could have used Arie as an excuse to see me off.

The other 'onderdijker' (Dutch word meaning dived-under) was Cor, a 22 year old ex-salesman, he was well educated and knew enough English to make conversation with me. He did not like farmwork and was always telling me of the social distinction between country and town folk. I soon knew everybody by name. I was very well treated and respected by all.

The children used to gabble away to me and I had to learn

the language fast, my answers were usually either "ya"or "nay".They were told that I came from the South of Holland (Limburg) where the accent is different to theirs, so not to worry if they could not understand me at times. I was given a Dutch name, Kees, the children called me 'Oom Kees' (Uncle Kees).

Gerrit, with the Barneveld group of the underground had it all arranged that the dozen or so parachutists and airmen that were in Holland would meet at the full moon, the end of the month, and attempt to cross the Rhine back to our forces in the South.

Patiently I waited until the end of January and then it snowed and snowed and snowed with the result that it was like daylight out at night and impossible to move without being seen. The operation was put off until the full moon at the end of February.

The underground boys watched every German movement along the route we were to take down to the river. Then two nights before we were due to move off something went wrong. Underground men were captured and the Germans in this area tightened up security.

I always carried a 9mm Browning automatic in my jacket pocket and one night as I went to bed I noticed it had gone. I told the 'governor', van Dijk, and said it must have been taken for it could not drop out. He went straight into the twins bedroom, two boys aged seven named Wim and Henk and asked them if they had it. There it was, under their pillow, they only wanted it to play with. While my jacket was on the back of the chair they had felt it in the pocket.

One Sunday morning at the end of January a policeman from Amersfoort came to visit the 'governor'. He was a well-known figure in the underground movement and the governor told him immediately about his English guest.

Van Goor, the policeman was a great big fellow, he violently shook me by the hand, sung praises of England and Englishmen all the morning. He had been a merchant sailor before the war and a frequent visitor to London. Proudly he showed me his watch that came from a well-known London watchmaker, his overcoat he was wearing was bought twelve years previously in Regent Street and was still good for many years, in fact anything that was from England was good.

Each province or county of Holland had its own organisation for the underground movement and I was just outside van Goor's area. This did not suit our policeman so he saw his chief and they came along one evening prepared to take me back to Amersfoort with them. The 'governor' said he had signed for me and before I could go he would have to get permission from Gerrit and the Barneveld group.

Gerrit was sent for and at 10 o'clock in the evening, arrived with a very worried expression. His answer was a plain and straightforward 'NO'. I was wanted by the Barneveld group, and I was to stay until I was wanted for the job in Barneveld, that I had previously been warned about.

After all this explanation Van Goor and his chief were not satisfied and said that Amersfoort was a more important town, that it was the other side of the 'water-line' (a natural defence line used in 1940) and all they required was me to make their plans complete.

This argument went on for an hour. I couldn't follow everything as a few swear-words crept in and both sides wanted to talk at once, so I said goodnight to everybody and retired.

The townspeople were very short of food and every Thursday a lady cycled 20 miles to collect some butter, milk, eggs and potatoes from us on the farm. Whenever this lady came I had to retire to my bedroom for the rest of the day as the farmer did not want too many people to know of my presence.

It often happened that when I slipped down to get my food, the lady, Mrs Willigers saw me. After about six weeks stay on the farm Mrs Willigers started asking questions as to my identity, she was put off by saying I was a deaf and dumb person. Her immediate reply was "He does not look deaf and dumb to me, he looks like an English soldier ".

I was immediately introduced and hearty greetings were exchanged all round. Mrs Willigers had a daughter named Betty who also wanted to meet the Englishman, so one

Thursday she cycled over with her mother and brought the weeks news in English to me.

Betty had a wireless set, and listened each morning to the BBC's news read at dictation speed. She copied it down, typed a copy each day and regularly brought the weeks news to me each Thursday. Before this I only had the news from the German controlled weekly newspaper and it put a different angle on affairs. In 1942 Betty's boyfriend had travelled across Belgium and France into Spain and managed to get to England and become a pilot with the RAF. She was only waiting for the end of the war so that she could marry him.

Her brother Cor was in hiding at home, he had once been taken away by the Germans to work in Germany. His mother on hearing from him had cycled to his address and as soon as he finished work one evening at the factory she cycled, with him on the carrier, all the way home - some 300 miles, such was the spirit of defiance towards the Germans.

About the beginning of March a nearby farmer said he could accept Cor as an 'onderjijker' and Cor dressed as a woman cycled with his sister from Bussum.

On the way the German soldiers had whistled at the 'girls' and Cor had great pleasure in cycling past and waving back to them.

By the end of March I had been seen about talking by so many people that it became common knowledge all around who I was, and everybody went out of their way to pass a 'goed-dag' and a knowing wink.

I started wandering off between meals visiting various farms where I was known and especially the home of an evacuated family from Amersfoort. Jack and Bram Nakman had a coal business in town but it had had to close down as there was no coal to sell. So instead of being another couple to work for the Germans they brought their wives with them and worked on the farm.

Another farm nearby had a railway driver as an 'onderdijker', he with the other railwaymen had orders from the underground movement to stop work in September 1944 and leave the railways useless to the Germans. These men were made an allowance of half pay to stay away from work by the underground.

On the 19th February I celebrated my twenty-first birthday and everybody wished me the equivalent of "Many happy returns ".

I had an egg for breakfast and then wandered off into our wood shed in the middle of a field and to read a book. The evening meal was at seven o'clock and afterwards we celebrated with cherry wine.

All sang something like "He's a jolly good fellow" and presents were given out. I received a 10 guilder note (about £1), a silver guilder (no longer made), 20 cigarettes and a birthday card. A few days later I was given a beautiful book mark made by a blind person. It was made with coloured silks and read 'HOLLAND 19-2-45 ". It is one of my most cherished souvenirs.

I had several near squeaks about this time and it did not help matters that a German company of soldiers had been billeted in the village. I was meandering in the farmyard at the back of the house one afternoon when two German Officers cycled straight up to me and let fly with a mouthful of German. I did not know whether to stand to attention, raise my hand and say "Heil Hitler" or do the most natural thing.

When the instructions or abuse had ended I gave them a most acknowledging nod and walked smartly away to fetch the 'governor' to see what they wanted. I thought I had better make myself scarce, so I retired into one of the hiding places we had in the house. By opening the floor of the cupboard in the best-room I could drop into the foundations of the farmhouse and nobody was any the wiser.

On another occasion I was reading a Phillips Oppenheim thriller just after lunch in the best-room, with the windows raised slightly at the bottom when my thoughts were shattered by a German soldier shouting at me through the open part of the window. I listened to what he had to say and heard the word "Aitches" mentioned which I knew to mean eggs. I closed my book and walked into the kitchen telling Mrs van Dijk to see to the soldier. Although we had plenty of eggs she would not let him have any.

Jans van Dijk          Johan van Dijk

The family van Djik from Achterveld with their fourteen children.
Six emigrated to New Zealand.

The German soldiers as well as the civilians were getting short of food by now as the RAF had complete command of the air. Hardly any transport was moving on the roads.

The governor managed to swap potatoes for paraffin and so we had a lamp and light during the evenings. Most houses just sat in darkness through these months.

It was during one of these evenings in late February we were sitting around the table playing cards when a commanding rat-tat-tat came on the outside door. We were barred and shuttered and nobody could get in. Again came the rat-tat-tat and "open-up" in German.

We three evaders, Jacob, Cor and myself made for the exits. I went into the next door bedroom and the other two went to the side entrance to let themselves out. I thought the Germans might have the place surrounded so thought I would hide in the building. There was no time to get into any of the hiding places so I quickly closed the door behind me and stood inside the dark bedroom with two children sleeping in one bed and nobody in the other.

My first thought was to hide under the bed, but the governor had made the bed frames himself and a plank of wood made the side only seven inches from the ground and I could not crawl under. By this time the voices had been raised in the next room and there seemed a furious argument going on. I stood by the door revolver in hand ready to shoot my way out if necessary, but I was hoping that the governor would tell him that his children were asleep in there.

I waited nervously fingering the trigger and it seemed ages waiting for something to happen, although it could have only been a matter of minutes. As there had been no firing out at the back I guessed that the other two had managed to get away so I started to open the shutters on the windows from inside.

The window creaked and groaned at every slight push and the shutters made a horrible noise. It was moonlight but I was in the shadows of the farmhouse, after looking around I went through the narrow 18 inch window head first and landed up in a heap on the ground. I made my way across the yard into the chicken-house and passed through a small door at one end into a hollow haystack that had been erected.

Inside we had a radio, but no electricity to run it, two bunks that were flea ridden and a torch. This was a safe hiding place from the Germans.

I waited about a half-hour and then the Governor came and said that "All is good" in English and told me of their visit. Apparently the Germans had a lot of stores to move in the morning and wanted our horse and cart and the governor to work for them. The governor explained that the cart was "Kaput" (broken) and the mare was with foal and must rest, but he would be pleased to turn up in the morning and help as he was the only male on the farm. Needless to say he did not attend in the morning.

Just after my birthday we found that our potatoes would not last until the new ones were ready for digging. Potatoes could be bought about 40 miles away in the north east of Holland but we had to provide our own transport. Van Dijk with his neighbour decided to go together with two horses, ours and his, pulling the biggest cart we had.

It would be quite a dangerous journey for the RAF were machine gunning everything moving on the roads during the day and there was the risk of the Germans commandeering the horses and cart. After the evening meal all the villagers turned out to wish them 'God-speed', it was quite an event.

Mrs van Dijk was very worried but on the fifth day they arrived safely back home with a huge load of potatoes.

The winter of 1944-45 was a hard one, it had started very wet and cold and January and February had seen inches of snow. By the beginning of March it looked as though we were to have a good Spring.

I used to take the children down to the brook that divided our farm from another and we paddled in the shallow end. I showed them how to build a bridge across the deep part and lower downstream put large stones in to make stepping stones. By the end of March every evening we went swimming with one person keeping a look-out for the Germans. One evening in late March we saw a terrific artillery barrage open up the final crossing of the Rhine into

Germany and we were disappointed that the army went eastwards into Germany instead of coming our way.

By this time the cows had calved and baby lambs and piglets were running about together. It was at this time that I saw my first lynching. A neighbouring dog had been worrying the sheep and slashed with its claws at the underside of a ewe that had just given birth. Blood spurted from the wound and the dog had to be destroyed. News of this happening spread like wildfire and in a few minutes about a dozen farm-hands armed with sticks were chasing this sheep-worrier.

They caught it after about twenty minutes and cut its throat. I had to walk away when I realised what was going to happen for not being used to this way of life it nauseated me.

The van Dijk family, like the majority of farmers in Achterveld, was a Roman Catholic one, and every month the Father of the Church came to visit each household. Whenever he came to us I had to keep well out of the way as he was unaware of my presence.

By the beginning of April we knew that the army was making in our direction. The RAF were continually flying over us, keeping watch on anything moving on the roads and firing at it, far too close to Achterveld to be healthy.

The Germans were looking for horses for transport as the troops in Holland were practically cut off from those in Germany.

One sunny afternoon I was reading a book in the wood-shed in the middle of a field, our mare was grazing outside, when across the field I noticed a soldier walking towards me.

I realised that I could not stay there as the German would want to speak to me if he entered. I walked out of the shed in the most nonchalant way I could muster, and went in the opposite direction. The soldier shouted something at me but I made out I did not hear, and continued walking down to the brook. Once down the bank I stopped to observe what the soldier had done but he was still looking in my direction. I took my clogs and socks off and waded across the stream. I found a well camouflaged dip in the copse near the stream and stayed there waiting.

I waited until I saw several soldiers move off from our farm-house and then made my way back to the house in a circular movement, moving away from the soldiers all the time.

All the time I kept the soldiers in view, keeping to the hedges as much as possible. When I was about 200 yards from the house I noticed that they were looking in my direction so I stood still up against a tree. A shot rang out, it was well wide of me but I dropped into a ditch and crawled as fast as I could to the chicken house and crept inside the haystack.

I had not seen anybody around the farmhouse so I had a problem thinking out what had happened.

After some time the governor came into the funk-hole and was all smiles. The Germans had been after our horse, but once again he had talked them out of it. He laughed as I dried my trousers.

We had no definite news of the progress of the Army, and at night could see the artillery barrage lighting the sky.

When the fighting came closer to us an unexploded shell landed on the next farm. Gingerly we dug it out and one of the farm-hands wanted it for a souvenir. It might still be ticking on his mantelpiece today!

Day by day in April we saw the Germans getting more and more worried, we had no idea which way we would be liberated but we just hoped that the Germans would retire from Achterveld without a fight.

Around the sides of the farmhouse we dug trenches to form some protection from the RAF. It is indescribable the optimism that the Dutch folk had that perhaps tomorrow or the next day they would be free after five years of frustration and occupation.

Every home had suffered under the Germans, thousands had died in concentration camps in Germany and thousands that had hidden at home had died of starvation.

Cats, dogs, goats and horses had all been killed for food in the towns and the doors in the houses had been burned for warmth. We British, who have never been occupied by the Germans have no idea what five years of the Gestapo and forced labour camps can mean.

By means of the underground bush telegraph we heard that the Canadians had crossed the River Ijssell, had reached the Zuider Zee and were making big strides in our direction.

During the afternoon of Tuesday April 16th, Cor Willegers went out on a long distance reconnaissance. He arrived back in the evening to say that the Germans were pulling out towards Amersfoort and the Army were nearing Barneveld.

We decided, Cor and I, to be off at day-break. That night I changed my clogs for shoes, cleaned my automatic, put a few souvenirs and some sandwiches in a small canvas bag, and meant to be away from it all, this time. I wore my battle-dress under a pair of blue dungarees.

We were up at 5am, and so was everybody else. The governor did not want us to go but thought it would be safer to wait for the Canadians to come to us.

Outside the farmhouse I said "Goodbye and thanks" to Johan van Dijk and his wife, Mina, Cor Post, Jacob and all the family. They gave us a send-off not unlike a Sunday School treat to the seaside.

It was about five miles to Barneveld and through the front-line so we had to move carefully. I told Cor that if anyone started shooting to look for cover and make a dive for it. We kept away from the roads and stuck to the edges of fields and bridle paths.

We gave a wide berth to all farmhouses, and anybody who looked like a soldier; and only had two false alarms in the first four miles.

A lady came over to us from a farmhouse and asked Cor what was happening as the Germans had been there last night but had moved away by this morning. Cor kept her well away from me and she fetched us a drink of water.

We had only progressed about another mile when I saw a jeep coming along this narrow side road.

In a few minutes we had ploughed into the copse by the side of the road and 'gone to earth'.

The jeep stopped about 50 yards from us and out stepped a sergeant with a revolver in his hand. It came to me then that he was in Canadian battle-dress. "Come on Cor," I yelled, "it's one of ours."

The officer watched me approach with caution. I pulled out my red beret and AB64 and told him that I was a parachutist and had been here since last September. A despatch rider came down the road and stopped by us. The sergeant of the 49th Loyal Edmonton Regiment, Canadian Army, told the despatch rider to take me on the back of his motorcycle to the HQ of the Battalion.

We moved like the wind into Barneveld and I met the Intelligence officer who asked me a few questions. On the way we passed tanks, bren gun carriers, wireless wagons, artillery and troops 'brewing-up' by the roadside.

It was mid-day by this time and I stayed with the Sergeants' mess for lunch.

Cor had made his own way into Barneveld and came and joined us. The Canadians gave me cigarettes by the hundred and I passed them over to the Dutchmen that were hanging around.

After lunch the Divisional General sent for me and I met him in a field outside Barneveld. He congratulated me on my evasion and asked me about German movements. I told him as much as I could, that the Germans were pulling out for Amersfoort and that a few were still in Achterveld that morning. I pointed the village out on his map and he told me of the close co-operation between land and air forces. He gave instructions for an aircraft to proceed to Achterveld and examine closely the church which was used as a look-out post, and the school-house where a company of Germans were billeted.

In a few minutes a plane from a forward fighter 'drome was on its way. Jokingly I asked him to order a plane to take me straight to London, but he said it was beyond his powers. I asked for some notepaper and wrote to my wife telling her I was safe and that I would be home shortly.

The Div. General said he was sending me back to Corps HQ and after receiving more cigarettes I went in a jeep back down the line. The jeep driver told me that Corps HQ was near Arnhem so I asked him to take me round the town for a ride.

I could not find the police building but I found the

Velperplein deserted. I wondered what had happened to everybody, whether they were safe, but the town was dead.

At Corps HQ I was given new underclothes, battle-dress, mug, knife, fork and spoon and a haversack, and then sent up to Almelo, a small town that had been liberated.

In a large private house I was introduced to about ten other chaps that had been 'on he run' like myself. There was one other airborne soldier, the others being all air-force men. Two were from the RAF and the rest consisted of Americans and a Pole.

Two bottles of whisky were put on the table and after a good meal we all tucked in and exchanged stories.

The other airborne solider was Major Sherriff of the Kings Own Scottish Borderers from Hayling Island. He fought at Arnhem and was shot through the arm by a revolver bullet in a hand-to-hand tussle with a German. His position was over-run and he was taken prisoner. Although handicapped with an injured arm, he escaped and joined the underground movement.

The two RAF chaps were David Ward from Melton Mowbray and Dave Blair from Malton, Yorkshire.

David Ward was with Transport Command and brought supplies over to the Resistance. In attempting to ensure that the supplies were dropped to the correct signal he flew too low and crashed into a tree.

The other chap had been on a bombing raid to Germany's industrial centre. He was shot down and had made his way back into Holland, he joined up with the underground movement, and waited for the liberation.

Some of the Americans at Almelo had slept in the haystack on Herman van Esveld's farm. Altogether there were so many stories and I had had such a busy and long day that I went to bed, and slept soundly, secure in the knowledge that I was the right side of the 'line', the first time for over seven months. The next morning was spent answering an oral interrogation, and then writing down as many place names that I could remember where I had stayed. The name of everybody that had helped me was wanted so that the people could be officially thanked.

After lunch we were taken to be medically examined, I was weighed and asked if I felt fit. I had to have this slip of paper before I could get home, so of course I felt fit.

All our papers were now in order, and the big question was: *WHEN do we go to England?*

At teatime we were told that a plane was taking us home the next day (Friday). The announcement was greeted with three cheers. An ENSA concert had been arranged in the town for that evening and we had seats if we wanted them.

Everyone had been issued with a new battle-dress but no badges of rank had been sewn on, so Pilot officer and Private walked along together to the concert.

The show was 'corny', but we laughed and clapped, knowing that by tomorrow we would be in England. That was all we thought of, England our home.

We arrived back at the billet and sandwiches were passed around, another bottle of whisky produced and when I retired to bed a party was just about to begin. Money could never buy the feeling of joy and exuberance that was with us that evening.

The next morning we four Englishmen said good-bye to the Yanks and the Pole and went by jeep through Arnhem, over the Bailey bridge beside the broken bridge where my troubles had started, and on to the aerodrome outside Nijmegen.

Here we waited, very impatiently, until six o'clock in the evening before our plane left. Our pilot took us across Belgium and France and showed us the beaches and fortifications along the coast. We sang all the way home, and one song I shall never forget is 'The White Cliffs of Dover' and this day it seemed particularly apt.

At Croydon airport the customs official asked me if I had anything to declare. This was one too many for my good spirits, so I asked him if he thought I had been on my holidays.

Here we received our postings, Major Sherriff and I to an ex-POW camp at Beaconsfield, and the two RAF chaps to the Air Ministry. A car took us to Marylebone Station and having ten minutes to spare I phoned a neighbour of my parents.

This neighbour thought she was speaking to a ghost as my letter had not yet arrived. I told her that I was at the station, that I was leaving in a few minutes and to tell my wife and parents that I hoped to be home in the morning.

My father on receiving the message, hastily and rather jumbled, went tearing off to Marylebone Station, I had already left for the camp, he asked if the porter had seen two soldiers, the porter said "yes" and that was all the satisfaction he had.

My father made straight for my wife's home and brought her from her bed at nearly midnight. Her immediate thoughts were that he had been drinking when he asked if I was at home, but over a cup of tea he told her all he knew, that I had phoned and said I was well and would be home in the morning.

This had been the first news of me since the note the previous October saying "Your husband is reported missing."

Meanwhile I had reported to the camp and gone to bed amongst chaps that had been POWs since 1940.

In the morning it was all haste to get home. A medical examination, forms to fill in, an interrogation, new kit to draw, rations, back pay and then home on leave.

I managed to get away at 10.30 am with a provisional six weeks leave and seven months back pay to come.

I came back to Marylebone Station by train then it was taxi all the way home to North London.

I had kept my door key with me, I opened the front door and walked up the stairs. My wife stood speechless on the landing. I hugged her and through her tears she smiled, relief had come to her mind after over seven months of anxiety.

I left my small pack at 2 Battalion HQ; the white house. While I went with Major Wallis 2 i.c. along the water front to find a boat.

126

The same scene after the battle. The road is cleared in 1945.
*Photos: Gemente Archiv Arnhem*

# The Roman Catholic church at
# Achterveld

For three weeks after I left, Achterveld was in a ten mile
area of no-man's-land. Both sides carried out active patrols
during the night and mines were laid. The church was
shelled one Sunday morning after I left.
The Germans had used the church as an observation tower.

# Epilogue

Although I was never taken prisoner by the Germans I was given the same six weeks leave period allocated to all returning prisoners. I think the truth of the matter was that the authorities had difficulty in finding a system to discharge their responsibilities to the many sick ex-servicemen who returned. I was given an extended period of leave and told to report to Gosforth Park, Newcastle with hundreds of ex-prisoners, many expecting to be given a medical discharge.

At my medical I was marked down as category B1 Malnutrition, fit to stay in the service.I was asked if I wished to stay with the Parachute Regiment or return to the Royal Armoured Corps, I had met my best friends in the Parachute Regiment and I wished to stay.

My posting was to the Parachute Infantry Training Depot at Bulford, once there Regimental Sergeant Major John Lord, MBE, told me I was to put up two tapes for a Corporal and attend an NCO's cadre on the Monday morning, on completion of the course I became a Drill Sergeant with a platoon of 30 new recruits for a 12 week induction course into the training and traditions of this new Regiment. (RSM Lord had been taken prisoner at Arnhem and had taken over guard mounting in the camp to show the Germans that we were a disciplined body of men despite being locked up).

You have read mention of Lieutenant Tom Ainslie the officer whom I accompanied on the patrol to find B company, when we could not make contact with them by wireless.

I had only been home in May for a couple of weeks when he called at my house to offer condolences to my wife, he had been told I was seen in the road dead, by the bridge.What a sensitive officer, he was returning two books I had left with his kit at Stoke Rochford. He was that overjoyed at seeing me alive he invited us to join him for lunch the next day at the Cafe Royal, Regent Street, in those days that was some invitation.

My mind was very concerned with the people who had been so kind to me in Holland during my enforced stay. I wrote to every name and address I could remember for news, the replies were worse that I could ever have imagined.

Johan Penseel my courier from the Police station and host for two months was in hospital at Arnhem having been found by the US army in the concentration camp at Ludwiglust, Germany. His two sons, John 25 and Martin 22 had died there in March, he had dug a grave and buried them.

The day after I left Arnhem on New Year's Eve, Johan was told by the Sicherheitdeinst to attend their office next morning with his two sons; Paul Bresser the journalist, told him to leave town but he said he would face them out. Johan, John and Martin attended and were sent to the concentration camp, the Germans knew about me. Johan Penseel later told me he thought we were given away by the nurse who asked Nico to get her over the Rhine and with whom Nico had slept the night, but not in Velperplein with me!

Johan never recovered his health although he lived to a good age. He was a section leader for the Arnhem LKP, I owe a lot to him.

That same day, 2nd January, Nico and Klaas had agreed to meet in the evening at a safe house in Arnhem, on arriving, Nico had difficulty in opening the front door, he tried the back entrance and walked into what he thought was an empty dark house and was confronted by a pistol at his chest. "Where have you Bob" came the snarl, "Er-um" and he was hit with an object. Nico quickly answered, "I saw him once but he went off."

Nico was subjected to torture, Klaas suffered the same, they were put in cars for the concentration camp in Germany. When they reached a wooded area they were told to get out and relieve themselves, they both thought they would be shot at that point, they were not and were taken on to the concentration camp at Neuengamme.

By February the camp was overfull with political prisoners and they were told they were to be moved, Klaas was suffering badly from dysentery and was not able to leave the camp, Nico left alone. Klaas was found dead in the camp when the US army arrived on 5th May, he was 25 years of age.

Nico was rescued by the US army at his camp at Wobbelin in May, eventually he was brought to the hospital at Arnhem, he stayed for several months, he never fully recovered. The Dutch army allowed him to join a Dutch Military Police customs unit at Emmerich on the Rhine, Germany.

In 1945 I was training young Paras but we had moved to Aldershot, I managed to get the Commanding Officer's permission for Nico to join me in the Barracks for two weeks, it was the highlight of his life. An excellent companion at all times, we enjoyed each others company, I miss him, he died some 12 years ago.

The Policeman who guided me through the town in Arnhem was Lieutenant Hans van Maris, he continued in the police service and ended his career as the Chief of Police at Zandvoort, I am still in contact with him and his family. The other officer who said he could not help me, was pro-German and he kept his word and did not report our meeting, his wife Mrs H ten Hove wrote to me after the war to ask if I would give him a reference for the War Crimes Tribunal, I agreed saying he did me no harm and did not give me away. I sent her that statement and he received a sentence of two and a half years in prison.

The very brave farmer H van Esveld of Kootwijkerbroek; with the servicemen in the hollow haystack, helped thirty or more British and US Airforce evaders back into safe hands, he lived until he was 88, what luck I had in finding such fine strong characters. After Klaas and Nico, Jan Himmerling took me around looking for a billet and then my next courier Gerrit van den Munkhof cycled with me trying to find someone who would take me in until I crossed the Rhine. They were all so very kind but every farmhouse we visited had evacuees from Arnhem with them. They all gave us coffee and a slice of rye bread.

Late in the afternoon on 3rd January we stopped to speak to Johan van Dijk, a small farmer, just outside the village centre of Achterveld. He was willing to take me, instead of the three days he was told I would stay, I stayed for three and a half months, never once was I made to feel unwanted, a wonderful family, with nine children at that time, Johan is 93 now and his wife Johanna died in 1999, a very brave and kind couple.

When I arrived he was hiding three Dutch evaders and an Austrian Jew. I did not know that such good people existed on this earth. For some years now, every Sunday morning I telephone the family in Holland, I have been made to feel I am part of that family.

At my interrogation by Military Intelligence, MI9 in London I named every person who had helped me, each one was rewarded with a certificate from our Government and the USA for their help given to escaped PoWs and evaders. The Dutch government gave each a commemorative medal, the Resistance Cross.

If caught by the Germans each one would have been shot out of hand, the farm burnt down, there was no trial or appeal system as we know it.

Every night when I retire to bed and climb into my clean sheets I think of the nights I slept rough in my army boots, 'on the run,' sleeping with one ear cocked listening for trouble.

# Appendix A

## Military situation at Arnhem

Below is part of the war diary of General Browning, Officer Commanding the Allied Airborne Operations in Holland. His Primary task; to capture the Arnhem Bridges. I have only used the information relevant to my story. General Horrocks, XXX Corps, was given the task of reaching he Rhine bridge at Arnhem. Expected time of arrival; under 48 hours.

**Sunday, 17 September.** North end of Arnhem Bridge held by 1 British Airborne. XXX Corps met stiffer opposition than was expected but managed to advance seven to eight miles of the 64 necessary.

**Monday, 18 September.** Fierce fighting at the bridge but holding. XXX Corps resumed the advance at 0600 hours to make Eindhoven, total mileage 13.

**Tuesday, 19 September.** Bridge still held at North end. Remainder of British Airborne slowly being cut off in small units. Four battalions, in addition to the one at the bridge, were out of touch and, except for a few, personnel never rejoined the Division. XXX Corps using a Grenadier Guards battalion with tanks combined with the 82nd American Airborne Division made an assault on the bridge at Nijmegen. It failed.
*(11 miles short of the target and already overdue.)*

**Wednesday, 20 September.** Small party still on the bridge. Division's casualties had been heavy and the troops were tired. XXX Corps by 1845 hours had captured Nijmegen railway bridge and the road bridge by 1930 hours.
*(Only 11 miles to go.)*

**Thursday, 20 September.** Arnhem bridge now in German hands. One Polish Parachute Brigade sent from England, they drop near Driel on the south side of the Rhine, south of the Division HQ at Oosterbeek, Germans control north bank. XXX Corps made every effort to advance but were held up after very little progress.
*(Still 11 miles short of Arnhem and that is in German hands).*

**Friday, 21 September.** Shrinking perimeter at Oosterbeek. Liaison officer from the Polish Brigade made contact at Oosterbeek. XXX Corps made contact with Poles at Driel at 0800 hours. A patrol of the Household Cavalry Regiment in armoured cars arrive. That night a few rafts carrying about 50 Poles and some food and ammunition could be got across.

**Saturday, 23 September.** British Airborne withstood heavy and continuous attacks with shelling and mortaring throughout the day. XXX Corps hoped to cross the river that night, but this proved impossible. At 2020 hours permission received to withdraw British Airborne from north of the Rhine if the position warranted.

**Sunday, 24 September.** Division now down to an effective strength of 2,000 men, quite incapable of a concerted movement . . . must be evacuated in small parties through enemy lines. XXX Corps managed to get up to 400 Dorsets across the river but they did not join up with the Airborne. No intention of attacking the Arnhem bridge, opposition too great and time too short.
*(What a difference this would have made to my story.)*

**Monday, 25 September.** They held out for yet another day. Evacuation started at 2200 hours. By dawn the following day, 2163 officers and men had been brought out. It had not been possible to bring the wounded with them.

**Tuesday, 26 September.** At 1130 hours permission was received for the Division to be flown home to England when ready.

Casualties: 1 British Airborne Division, all causes 6462. British Glider Pilots 738. Some 180 men of the 4 Dorsets were left on the north bank of the Rhine, acting as a covering party.

The second Battalion The Parachute Regiment, commanded by Lt. Col. J. D. Frost DSO, MC, went to Arnhem with 501 officers and men, not one officer and only 17 men were counted when the Division evacuated on the 26th September. The smallest number to return of any of the Parachute battalions.

DURING one of my visits to the Public Record Office at Kew, I came across the following report. PRO CAB 106/1111. It is called McGregors Diary and on enquiry I was told he was a senior RAF Officer, part of the intelligence group on the combined team stationed at Moor Park for Allied Airborne operations. It is a most enlightening report.

I quote:

> '26 September 1944. A short signal from War Office this morning says that 1st Division has been withdrawn - believed about 800 survivors. So 'MARKET' has failed and the agony is ended - and what was, perhaps, the finest Division this country has ever produced has been almost wiped out.'

Why did the operation fail? It failed for two major reasons:

1. The Air Plan was bad. All experience and common sense pointed to landing all three Airborne Divisions in the minimum period of time, so that they could form up and collect themselves before the Germans reacted. All three Divisions could have been landed in a space of 12 hours or so, but FAAA insisted on a plan which resulted in the second lift (with half the heavy equipment) arriving more than 24 hours after the Germans had been alerted. All this evidence seems to point to the fact that this second lift was disorganised or destroyed by the enemy on arrival. Hence, the 1st Division had to fight its battle without a really effective Glider Brigade - a hopeless task.

Who was responsible for this plan which seemed even at the time to be highly dangerous, because it ignored so many of the lessons already learned about airborne. First Allied Airborne Army must take the main responsibility for they settled the plan against advice. FAAA, that unnecessary Headquarters, composed mainly of people who have no experience of airborne or troop carrier, yet given this ghastly power over the lives of the best troops and aircrews U.S. or England can produce.

2. The Ground Army was late on its time-table. Some people in 21 Army Group and below must have underestimated

the difficulties of the ground advance to Arnhem for the Ground Forces were several days late in arrival - in fact they never really arrived in sufficient strength to relieve 1st Division. Considerable blame must attach to the planners, and possibly the Commanders and troops, connected with this failure - but I consider the degree of blame less than under (1) because I have always thought an Airborne Division ought to be able to hold out for eight to ten days if it is dropped effectively and is kept supplied. So, if the 1st Division had been dropped effectively, and the air had kept it supplied, I believe it would have held out strongly for eight days, and the operation could have succeeded. Four days is a reasonable period to aim at for relief, but in emergency this should be doubled.

Arnhem need not have failed. That it did is due to putting inexperienced people in charge of a highly complicated operation. In civil life, such a failure would result in immediate dismissal; in Russia, it would result in court martial; in Allied democracy, it results in nothing.

No one has the courage to speak openly or to act.

*The author: I cannot think of a better ending to the story than this highly informed review of the failure. The Divisional General, Major General Roy Urquhart, DSO, was NOT given the award he deserved for his part in the operation. The Dutch Government awarded him their Bronze Lion medal. It was he who organised the evacuation of the survivors against great odds. An excellent soldier, much admired by his men.*

# Appendix B

M.I.9/PW/7/8483.

14362066 Pte. PEATLING, R.W.,


    You will undoubtedly be very pleased to hear that your diary has turned up, having been found at the house of a Dutch Farmer - namely H. Van Esveld, Dwarsqiafweg 5, Essen, BARNEVELD by an officer of the 1st Canadian Division.

    I am taking care of it pending your instructions as to where you would like it to be sent. Your dedication is most appropriate and I am sure your wife and father will be most interested in your first class evasion.

    While waiting for your present address I have read it and must congratulate you.


M.I.9,
Room 327,
Hotel Victoria,
Northumberland Avenue,
LONDON, W.C.2.

5 August 1945.

Lieut.-Colonel, G.S.

137

# Appendix C

On the 31st.October 1944 whilst an evader in Arnhem, after the evacuation of the British Forces, I was discovered alone and hungry by a Police Officer, Lt.H.ten Hove and his comrade Lt.H.van Maris, both of the Arnhem Police Force. Lt.ten Hove immediately informed me that he was a member of the National Socialist Movement and as such should not help me in any way. Nevertheless he gave me cigarettes and his manner was friendly. He also provided me with information of the movement of British Forces and gave me news of events in this theatre during the previous six weeks of which I knew nothing. He made it quite clear that he would not interfere with me being there provided I did not indulge in any subversive activities. He explained to me that he was neither pro-German nor pro-British but had only the interest of his own country at heart.

When he left, we shook hands, wished me luck and hoped for my safe return to my wife, as he said he quite understood my feelings in wishing to get home.

Lt.ten Hove said he could not return, but he was fully aware that Lt.van Maris would be returning.

Lt.van Maris did return and finally helped me to escape.
Lt.ten Hove in no way interfering. Consequently I was able to remain in Holland and assist the Dutch Resistance Movement in the use of British weapons.

It is my opinion that Lt.ten Hove acted as he thought best solely in the interest of his own country. He could quite easily have turned me over to the Germans yet while he did not actively assist in my escape, he placed no obstacle in my path.

21/8/46

*R.W.Peatling*

Corporal.

138

## CERTIFICATE

This is to testify that Pte. Peatling R.W. who was my batman in 2nd. Bn. The Parachute Regiment is in my opinion a most suitable candidate for a commission. He was a very useful member of the Signals Platoon and his bearing in action was exemplary. He has excellent qualities of responsibility and initiative which is passed by the fact that following the action at Arnhem he lived for three months in that town and later with Dutch forces in the country until the liberation of Holland by allied forces. During this time he performed most useful work in teaching English and instructing Dutch partisans in weapon training. I am of the opinion therefore that every consideration should be given to his application.

J.T. Ainslie ft.

7 June 1945     The Parachute Regt.

# Expenses incurred whilst escaping — official.

Ref:- ME/TGP/2604.

1436206b.
Pte...Pershing...R.W.

..............................

With reference to the claim made by you at the Repatriation Camp

for .....Expenses...incurred...whilst...escaping.....

........................................................

will you please note that it has been found necessary to refer the
matter to the War Office. Some time may elapse before a reply can be
expedited, but you will be notified immediately a decision is given.

*[signature]*............ Lieut,

for NEGIMENTAL PAYMASTER,

Howbhill Avenue,
EDINBURGH. 7.
6 - 1945.

NBJ.

**. . . and eighteen months later came the reply!**

TO: Officer Commanding,

"C" Coy.

No.1. PARA. REGT.
I.T.C.

ORDERLY ROOM
No.1 PARA REGT.
30 JAN 1947
Ref. ........
I INFANTRY TRAINING CENTRE

NE/REP/ 2604

No. 14368066. Rank Pte. Name ....PEATLING. R. Unit ...R.A.C.:...
Repatriated Prisoner of War. EX GERMANY

Please interview the above-named soldier and inform him that his account has been credited with the sum of £ 1 : 3 : 9 ; which represents 10 guilders converted at 2/9 > and 10 R. Marks converted @ 6' each = 5/- in full settlement of his claim for informations incurred whilst so-ray

The above reference should be quoted in any query on this subject.

Hawkhill Avenue,
EDINBURGH. 7.
11 194 .

W. Hall
Lieut.

for REGIMENTAL PAYMASTER.

ARMY PAY OFFICE.
EDINBURGH
28 JAN 47

141

Martin and John Penseel were captured two days after
I left Arnhem. They died at Mecklenberg concentration camp.

Mr & Mrs J Penseel meet their wartime evader at
the 1946 Arnhem pilgrimage; seventeen months after
Mr. Penseel's release from the concentration camp
where he had buried both his sons.